THE BASIS OF
TRADITIONAL CHINESE
MEDICINE

The Basis of Traditional Chinese Medicine

Shen Ziyin and Chen Zelin

SHAMBHALA

BOSTON & LONDON

1996

Shambhala Publications, Inc.
Horticultural Hall
300 Massachusetts Avenue
Boston, Massachusetts 02115

©1994 The Commercial Press (Hong Kong) Ltd.

Translators: Tian Peiming, Zhang Kai, Cai Jingfeng
Scientific and Translation Editor:
Fung Kam-Pui, MB, BS, MRCP (UK), FRCPE

Published by agreement with
The Commercial Press (Hong Kong) Ltd.

9 8 7 6 5 4 3 2 1

First Shambhala Edition
Printed in the United States of America

∞ This edition is printed on acid-free paper that meets
the American National Standards Institute Z39.48 Standard.

Distributed in the United States by Random House, Inc.,
and in Canada by Random House of Canada Ltd

Library of Congress Cataloging-in-Publication Data

Shen, Tzu-yin.
    The basis of traditional Chinese medicine/Shen Ziyin and
Chen Zelin.
        p. cm.
    Originally published: Hong Kong: Commercial Press, c1994.
    ISBN 1-57062-192-6 (alk. paper)
    1. Medicine, Chinese. I. Ch'en, Tse-lin. II. Title.
R602.S478   1996   96-15548
610'.951—dc20   CIP

FOREWORD

Traditional Chinese Medicine (TCM) has a history of over three thousand years, and has been developed almost entirely free from the influence of the Western world. Over the centuries, it has been proven to be efficacious and has provided cures for both acute diseases and chronic illnesses. It is still practised widely in China and Chinese communities all over the world, including localities where Western medicine is the mainstream of medical practice, such as in Hong Kong.

In Western countries, many people have heard of traditional Chinese medicine, but generally only in regard to acupuncture, which has been used to a small degree in the West in recent decades. Herbal medicine has also become increasingly interesting to Westerners who wish to take fewer pills and have more control over their own health care. However, these two areas are only a part of TCM, and do not explain the theoretical basis behind it, or how it actually works.

This book attempts to introduce the general reader to the fundamental concepts and workings of TCM in a way that the layman can easily understand. TCM has a great deal to offer to the Western world. Although some of the ideas may be quite foreign, TCM is without doubt worthy of attention, study and research. We hope that this book will help readers see the enormous contributions that can be made by TCM, and will bring people to a greater understanding of the Chinese view of medicine and healing.

CONTENTS

1

A BRIEF HISTORY OF THE DEVELOPMENT OF TRADITIONAL CHINESE MEDICINE

The history of Traditional Chinese Medicine (TCM) can be traced back to approximately three thousand years ago, when the Chinese first developed a written language. At that time, prior to the first recorded dynasties, information about infectious diseases, as well as various medical and surgical techniques, were inscribed on bones or turtle shells. Later, when people wrote on strips of bamboo, medical information was naturally included.

Fig. 1.1 Examples of an ancient bone and a bamboo strip with inscriptions

In the Spring and Autumn Period (770–475 B.C.) and the Warring States Period (475–221 B.C.) immense changes took place in manufacturing, with the invention of iron casting and metal technology. During this time, medical practice advanced on par with the concomitant socio-cultural and scientific achievements. Knowledge built on previous records was assimilated and the new techniques developed for manufacturing were put to use in the medical field.

The first academic work which summarized the theories of TCM and described clinical experiences was the *Nei Jing*, often translated as *The Yellow Emperor's Inner Canon of Medicine* (*nei* means internal and *jing* means text, or classic book). Although it is attributed to the Yellow Emperor (Huang Di), who lived about 4,000 years ago, it was actually compiled by various authors throughout several dynasties based on previous records. In 18 volumes, it is the earliest complete book on TCM, and expounds the interrelation between human beings and nature, one of the basic tenets of TCM. It also discusses the basic theories of the pathology, diagnosis, prevention and treatment of various diseases, and is considered the "bible" of TCM.

The philosophy of Taoism also played a large part in the development of TCM, as seen in the fact that the *Nei Jing* strongly emphasized the importance of balance of one's mental and physical states. Having a calm mind and not indulging in excess of any kind were considered prerequisites for good health. This idea comes from the Taoist concept of *yin* and *yang* (which will be discussed in more detail in the next chapter), and the natural balance of all things in the universe. It is interesting to note that in recent times in the West, such considerations as one's state of mind have been taken more and more into account when treating patients.

Acupuncture was first practised over 2,200 years ago,

by a physician named Bian Que (pronounced *"chuey"*). He also developed the method of diagnosing a patient using the four techniques of observation, listening, questioning and palpation, now accepted as the standard in TCM. Bian Que was greatly respected as a gynecologist, pediatrician and gerontologist, having mastered many therapeutic methods now commonly used. In addition, he is generally considered to be the author of a text called the *Nan Jing* (*nan* means difficult or perplexing) which described treatment for diseases traditionally difficult to cure.

In the second century A.D., a physician named Hua To, often referred to as the God (or Father) of Surgery, performed the first surgical operations using anesthesia made from herbs. He also created a series of exercises based on the posture of five animals, the tiger, deer, bear, monkey and bird. He based these exercises on the Chinese saying that running water cannot stagnate, just as human beings must move to stay healthy. These five postures indeed form

Fig. 1.2 A drawing of Hua To

the basis of what is now known as *Tai Ji Quan* (commonly referred to in the West as *tai-chi*), a gentle set of movements often practised by elderly people to keep fit.

Fig. 1.3   Practising *tai ji quan* (*tai-chi*)

Also in the second century, a man named Zhang Zhong-jing wrote several classic texts, including one devoted entirely to diseases caused by the cold, a treatise on fever, a book on household remedies and a synopsis of prescriptions of various herbal medicines. Based on the *Nei Jing*, he classified infectious diseases into six symptomatic types with treatment tailor-made to each. His work pioneered the clinical approach to diagnosis, symptom analysis and prescription.

One of the main diagnostic tools in TCM is feeling the brachial pulses, a technique known as palpation. In the third century A.D. the *Mai Jing* (*mai* means pulse) was written by Wang Shu-he, considered the first expert on the pulse method of diagnosis. This important work was translated into several languages and was introduced to Japan and Korea as early as the sixth century.

The discovery and application of Chinese herbs and drugs has an extremely long history. The earliest pharmacopoeia in China, called *Herbology* was compiled in the second to third centuries A.D., although it is often attributed to Shen Nong, a legendary emperor who lived some 5,000 years ago. *Herbology* summarized the cumulative knowledge of herbal medicine up to that time. Three hundred and sixty-five drugs were classified into three categories according to their uses and applications. By the fifth century a renowned pharmacologist named Tao Hong-jing had added another 365 new drugs, published in his *Commentaries on Shen Nong's Herbology*.

Fig. 1.4　A drawing of the legendary Shen Nong

During the Sui and Tang Dynasties (581–907 A.D.) medical science saw rapid developments, with voluminous and comprehensive medical works available. In 659 A.D. four scholars were assigned by an emperor of the Tang Dynasty to edit a book called the *Newly Compiled Materia*

Medica, in which they elaborated on existing material. This book described 114 new drugs, bringing the total to 844 varieties, and was the first official pharmacopoeia sponsored by the imperial government. In the 10th to 12th centuries, with the invention of printing, the government issued a text called *Classified Materia Medica for Emergencies*, which listed 1,746 types of medicines.

Great advances were made in the 12th and 13th centuries (the Song and Yuan Dynasties) by four leading physicians. Liu Wan-su did work in the area of *hot* and *cold* diseases, based on the concept that weather and environment affect health. He suggested that *hot* diseases should be treated with *cold* medicines and vice versa, to counteract their confronting effects. He proposed that there is virtually always an element of *fire* in the latter stages of a disease. Therefore medicines of a *cold* nature should be used to help the healing process. His practice is known as the "Cold" school of medical thought. Another doctor named Zhang Zi-he suggested that exogenous *evils* in the body must be expelled (more will be discussed on this later) in treatment, thus he used drastic drugs like purgatives and diaphoretics. He founded the "Purgation" school of medical thought.

The third great physician of that time, Li Dong-yuan, emphasized the importance of the spleen and stomach, through which nutrients are absorbed. By restoring the functions of the spleen and stomach with the use of certain drugs, the recovery of illnesses was found to be accelerated. Around the same time, Zhu Dan-xi discovered in his practice that *yang* was often in excess of *yin*, and thus suggested using drugs that would nourish the *yin* principle. These four physicians' unique research contributed significantly to the development of TCM.

The last historically important person to be discussed lived in the Ming Dynasty (1368–1644), and is considered China's greatest naturalist. Li Shi-zhen spent 40 years completing his comprehensive original work called the *Compendium of Materia Medica*, which was published in 1578. This classic, listing 1,892 drugs, is a synopsis of the experiences and theoretical knowledge of doctors up to the 16th century. A vast encyclopedia of herbs that is still used as reference today, it included 10,000 different prescriptions. Li Shi-zhen's work has exerted substantial influence on pharmacology and the spread of the use of Chinese herbs in the rest of the world.

 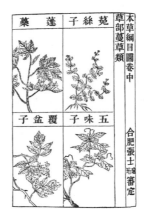

Fig. 1.5   A drawing of Li Shizhen and a page from his book the *Compendium of Materia Medica*

Since the founding of the People's Republic of China in 1949, a new approach to medical care has been used, combining both TCM and Western medicine, to excellent effect. As neither system has all the answers to every medical problem, it is therefore logical to utilize the best of both systems to improve health care for all. The following chapters will outline some of the major contributions of TCM to our general understanding of medicine.

2

YIN-YANG AND THE FIVE ELEMENTS

Yin-yang and the *five elements* are the fundamental principles of TCM. They are a consolidation of the experiences by which the complex physiology and pathology of the human body can be elucidated in simple terms.

The Theory of *Yin-Yang*

The ancient Chinese believed that every object in nature consists of two opposite yet complementary aspects, which combine to create a whole unit. *Yin* and *yang* represent the negative and positive principles of the universe, and are in constant flux. *Yin* and *yang* are also the principles underlying Chinese philosophy and metaphysics, and can in fact be applied to everything in the world.

Through repeated tests and long-term observation, it was proven that indeed this theory can be applied to all things, animate and inanimate, including, naturally, human beings. As a product of the universe, the human physiological functions comprise the *five elements* and *yin* and *yang*.

Fig. 2.1   A diagram of the *yin* and *yang* in equilibrium

When applied to medical studies, *yin* and *yang* are of the greatest importance. As the *yin-yang* symbol suggests, balance and harmony are the keys. In simple terms, when *yin* and *yang* are thrown off balance, disease can easily occur. As discussed in the previous chapter, herbal treatments always take this into consideration.

The concept of *yin-yang* is abstract but comprehensive. Dynamic, positive, bright, warm, solid and functional attributes are defined as *yang* while static, negative, dark, cold, liquid and inhibiting attributes are characterized as *yin*. Thus the sun is *yang* while the moon is *yin*; the sky is *yang* while the earth is *yin*; daytime is *yang* while nighttime is *yin*; fire is *yang* while water is *yin*. Sunlight and fire are hot while moonlight and water are cool. By analogy, warm elements are classified as *yang* and cold elements are taken as *yin*. Fire is dynamic and tends to ascend and is therefore treated as *yang*. Water is relatively static and tends to flow down. Thus elements that are active and ascending are described as *yang* whereas their counterparts being static and descending are described as *yin*. These are the characteristics of *yin* and *yang*. The following table shows some examples of the *yin-yang* classification:

Table 1 Relativity and Properties of *Yin and Yang*

Yin	Yang	Yin	Yang
moon	sun	inhibited	excited
earth	sky	retrogressive	progressive
night	day	hypoactive	hyperactive
cold	hot	passive	active
water	fire	hidden	apparent
winter	summer	interior	exterior
turbid	clear	downward	upward
static	dynamic	liquid	vapour

As shown in Table 1, *yin* and *yang* may refer to real matters as well as abstract ideas, and may describe virtually anything. *Yin* and *yang* are complementary to and interdependent of each other, yet they are opposite to their counterpart. Being related, they can be transformed to their opposite component under certain conditions. *Yin* and *yang* coexist with reference to each other. *Yin* exists because *yang* is present. *Yin* may emerge from *yang* and vice versa. This idea may be illustrated by the *yin-yang-yin* cycle. Functional activities in the human body (*yang*) are supported by the body fluids (*yin*). This produces nutrients (*yin*) which support the functional activities (*yang*). Similarly, functional failure of the internal organs (*yang*) jeopardizes the digestion of food into usable nutrients (*yin*).

The water cycle is a good example of *yin-yang* transformation. The water on earth (*yin*) vaporizes to gas form (*yang*); which after condensation to water (*yin*), falls down on earth again. In TCM terms, one can sometimes witness the transformation of *yin* and *yang* in a diseased patient. For example, if a patient has pneumonia, the symptoms tend to be *yang* symptoms, such as a high fever, restlessness, a flushed face, dry lips and a rapid pulse. If the infection should be complicated by septic shock for example, the symptoms change and become more *yin*-related, i.e. cold limbs, pallor, profuse sweating and a weak pulse. Similarly, a patient with *yin* symptoms overtreated with *hot*-natured drugs may show *yang* symptoms.

Yin and *yang* conditions do not remain in a static state. They are in perpetual dynamic equilibrium according to the patient's changing environment. It is this equilibrium of *yin* and *yang* that balances the production and regeneration of *qi* (energy), *blood* and the *body fluids* to maintain the healthy physiological functions of the body. This is called "the warning and waxing of *yin* and *yang*" in TCM. These theories are utilized to analyze clinical manifestations. A condition of *yang* excess, as in patients with a high fever, may be complicated by a *yin deficiency* as shown by dehydration or *fluid deficiency*. On the other hand, patients who feel very weak may have a *yang deficiency,* and will therefore be averse to the cold (*yin*).

The Application of *Yin-Yang* in Human Anatomy and Physiology

Yin-yang may also describe the relative positioning of the organs with reference to interior or exterior, anterior or posterior as well as inferior or superior. The back, being relatively external to the abdomen, pertains to *yang*. In TCM, the five *zang* (*solid*) organs (heart, liver, spleen, lung and kidney) are referred to as *yin* organs, while the six *fu* (*hollow*) organs (gallbladder, stomach, large intestine, small intestine, bladder and the *sanjiao*) are the *yang* organs. In addition, the five *zang* organs may be subclassified into *yin* and *yang* among themselves. The heart and lung located in the upper part of the body are the *yang* organs whereas the liver and kidney, being in the lower part, are the *yin* organs. Even an individual *zang* and *fu* organ may be divided into *yin* and *yang* subsets such as *heart yin* and *heart yang*, or *kidney yin* and *kidney yang* (refer to Chapter 3). Hence *yin* and *yang* are relative and flexible terms. Their implications may vary with different objects and phenomena.

The Application of *Yin-Yang* in the Illustration of Human Diseases

The *yin-yang* principle is used for explaining the mechanism of diseases. In TCM context, the healing and life-giving properties of *qi* protect the body against pathogenic or disease-causing factors. The latter may be further classified as *yin* and *yang* pathogenic factors. Diseases caused by *yin* factors may result in a preponderance of *yin* and thereby give rise to the *cold* syndrome. On the contrary, *yang* factors may cause a preponderance of *yang* and may result in the *heat excess* syndrome. The anti-pathogenic *qi* is generally divided into *yang qi* and *yin fluid*. In the case of a *yang qi* deficiency, the *cold deficiency* syndrome may occur, while in case of a *yin fluid* deficiency, the *heat deficiency* syndrome may appear. Therefore, all disease mechanisms may be deduced in terms of TCM concepts, such as "having an imbalance of *yin* and *yang*", "a *yang deficiency* leading to *external cold* and a *yin deficiency* leading to *internal heat*" and "a *yang excess* bringing about *heat*, while a *yin excess* bringing about *cold* ".

Extreme deficiency of either *yin* or *yang* may cause an insufficiency of its counterpart. Finally, there may be deficiency of both *yin* and *yang*. In the course of certain chronic illnesses, it is not uncommon to witness insufficient *yin fluid* production due to *yang deficiency* or on the contrary, a deficiency of *yin fluid* may jeopardize the generation of *yang qi*.

The Application of *Yin-Yang* in the Diagnosis of Diseases

Tipping the balance of *yin* and *yang* triggers off diseases and accounts for their progress. No matter how variable their clinical manifestations are, the fundamentals of diseases may be discussed and analysed in terms of *yin* and *yang* complexes or syndromes. The eight principal syndromes commonly used in TCM in clinical diagnosis and management are based on *yin* and *yang*. *Exterior* syndrome, *heat* syndrome and *excess* syndrome all denote *yang*, while *interior* syndrome, *cold* syndrome and *deficiency* syndrome denote *yin*. The importance of identifying *yin* and *yang* is evident from a quotation from the *Nei Jing*: "A skilful clinician differentiates between *yin* and *yang* first after inspecting the [patient's] facial features and feeling the pulse".

The Application of *Yin-Yang* in the Treatment of Diseases

The causes and manifestations of diseases, as already stated, are due to an excess or deficiency of either *yin* or *yang*. Once the nature of the disease pertaining to either *yin* or *yang* is assessed, the *yin-yang* balance should be restored through regulation. This is fundamental to treatment in TCM. Thus *yin-* and *yang*-natured herbs are used to treat diseases with *yang* and *yin* natures respectively. This is why herbs of a *cold* nature are prescribed for diseases of the *hot* type while herbs of a *warm* nature are chosen for diseases of the *cold* type. The *Nei Jing* says, "Monitor the *yin* and *yang* and regulate them until equilibrium is achieved. Warm the *cold*. Fill up any *deficiency* and purge the *excess*."

The properties, flavours and effects of traditional Chinese herbs can also be generalized in terms of *yin* and *yang*. For instance, herbs of a *cold* nature, or those that have a moistening effect, denote *yin*, while *warm*, *hot* and *dry* herbs denote *yang*; drugs bitter and sour in taste denote *yin*, while those pungent or sweet in flavour denote *yang*. Drugs with astringent and *descending* effects denote *yin*, while those with *ascending* and dissipating effects denote *yang*. In general, herbs with a *yin* nature are able to dampen the *heat* in a person and can dissipate the *internal heat* and hyperactive symptoms. Herbs of a *yang* nature are able to cause stimulation and excitation, and can thus promote the bodily functions and eliminate the involutional symptoms. The purpose of drugs is, therefore, to rectify the excess or deficiency of *yin* or *yang* and restore the equilibrium of the human body in order to achieve the healing effects.

The Theory of the *Five Elements*

The *five elements*, metal, wood, water, fire and earth are familiar to all people, and are part of our daily lives. The ancient Chinese, from their experiences, noted that these elements might be transformed into a wide variety of matters after processing. They therefore formulated the concept that these *five elements* are the basic composition of the universe and classified all matters and phenomena into the five respective elements according to their properties. The *five elements* are abstract terms which may refer to all concrete matters. Henceforth the theory of *five elements* has become a means used to systematize and categorize matters and phenomena in order to understand their mutual relations and changes.

The Law of Mutual Promotion and Subjugation

The theory of the *five elements* tries to explore nature and matters and their interrelations through the concept of "mutual promotion and subjugation". Mutual promotion infers that the *five elements* may activate, generate, help and potentiate each other. It is through these interpromotions of the elements that the *five elements* continue to survive, rejuvenate and transform. By the law of mutual promotion, therefore: wood promotes fire, fire promotes earth, earth promotes metal, metal promotes water, water promotes wood, and wood again promotes fire. The idea of "wood promotes fire" is easy to understand, as fire is created when wood is burned. Fire leaves ash (earth) behind after burning and hence "fire promotes earth". All metals are mined from earth or ore. Metals liquefy on heating, and on the other hand metallic utensils cause the surrounding cold moist air to condense into water drops. Trees and vegetation grow only when there is water, and will wither otherwise. Hence the statements "metal promotes water" and "water promotes wood" were derived.

In the law of mutual subjugation, "subjugation" means restraining, controlling and overcoming. It refers to mutual restraint, mutual control, and mutual overcoming within the *five elements*. It is through this restraint, which reinforces the balance of the *five elements*, that none of the elements are able to dominate the others. The law of subjugation governing the *five elements* is as follows: wood acts on earth; earth acts on water; water acts on fire; fire acts on metal; metal acts on wood; wood in its turn acts on earth.

The concept probably originated from simple observations of nature. The ancient Chinese saw trees growing on earth, impoverishing the soil, hence they concluded that "wood acts on earth". They built dams with earth to prevent floods, hence they concluded that "earth acts on water". Water puts out fire and hence "water acts on fire". Metals can be softened and melted by fire, hence "fire acts on metal". A sword or axe made of metal can fall a tree, hence "metal acts on wood". Figure 2.2 shows the mutual promotion and subjugation relationships.

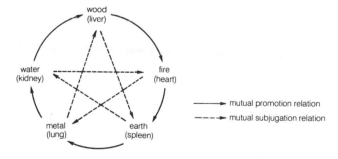

Fig. 2.2   Diagram showing the mutual promotion and subjugation relations among the five elements

A metaphorical description of the concept of mutual promotion is the mother-child relationship. Each of the *five elements* bears the possibility of promoting and being promoted by the respective counterpart. The mother produces the child. The element which promotes acts as the mother whereas the son is the one being promoted. Similarly, any of the *five elements* may restrain or dominate the other. Hence in the concept of mutual subjugation, we can relate an element either to one which subjugates or is being subjugated by the other.

Under abnormal situations, an element may push the law of mutual subjugation to the extreme. For instance, the wood element tends to subjugate the earth element. However, an excess of earth may weaken the wood element. This is called the phenomenon of counteraction. Conversely, the law of mutual subjugation may be reversed when the subjugating element is weak. For example, if there is a deficiency of the wood element and an excess of the earth element, earth, which is normally submissive to wood, may become the dominating element. This is the phenomenon of counter-restraining.

The Applications of the Theory of the *Five Elements*

The theory of the *five elements* is as widely applied as the theory of *yin-yang* in TCM regarding both diagnosis and treatment. It is mainly applied in the following two aspects.

All natural events and phenomena, as well as the *zang-fu* organs of the human body, are ascribed to one of the *five elements* according to their functions, physical properties and manifestations, as seen in Table 2. Thus we are able to analyze the relations between individual *zang-fu* organs, between the *external* body and *internal zang-fu* organs, and between the human body and nature in terms of the *five elements*. As depicted in Table 2, the liver is analogous to wood for its harmonious, flourishing and mild properties. The *heart yang* warms the whole body and it is analogous to fire. The spleen is responsible for assimilation of nutrients and corresponds with the earth. The *lung qi* is clear and descending, so it is analogous to metal. The kidney is analogous to water and it is responsible for storing the essence and regulating fluids in the body.

Table 2 The Five Categories of Things Classified according to the *Five Elements*:

Five elements	Wood	Fire	Earth	Metal	Water
Five directions	East	South	Middle	West	North
Five seasons	Spring	Summer	Late Summer	Autumn	Winter
Five environmental factors	Wind	Summer heat	Dampness	Dryness	Cold
Five colours	Green	Red	Yellow	White	Black
Five tastes	Sour	Bitter	Sweet	Pungent	Salty
Five *zang* organs	Liver	Heart	Spleen	Lung	Kidney
Five *fu* organs	Gallbladder	Small intestine	Stomach	Large intestine	Bladder
Five sense organs	Eye	Tongue	Mouth	Nose	Ear
Five tissues	Tendon	Vessel	Muscle	Skin & Hair	Bone
Five emotions	Anger	Joy	Meditation	Grief	Fear

In Table 2, those under the same column are related to one another and should be considered as a whole during clinical management. Anything associated with a disease in the liver calls for attention to the eye, tendon and the emotion of anger. These associations often have practical clinical implications. In TCM, drugs for the liver may be very useful in treating eye problems. The liver affects the tendons and is related to anger. Great anger which harms the liver is common in diseases. The liver pertains to wood, which flourishes in spring, so *liver yang* diseases are prevalent in spring. These phenomena, as summarized in Table 2, illustrate that the theory of the *five elements* systemizes the mutual relationship between the human body, the seasons, environmental factors, different tastes, the sense organs and the five tissues for the cognition of the unification between human beings, the organs and nature.

The mutual promotion and subjugation relations, according to the theory of the *five elements*, exist between the *zang-fu* organs in the human body. As shown by the rows in Table 2, the kidney essence (water) nourishes the liver (wood). The latter stores blood and supplies it to the heart (fire) which warms the spleen (earth). The spleen assimilates the essence of food to nourish the lung (metal) which clears the sweat for excretion through the skin and sends the fluid down to the kidney (water) for urine production. This illustrates the mutual promotion of the five *zang* organs. Conversely, the *lung qi* (metal) attenuates hyperactivity of the *liver yang* so that harmony of the liver (wood) is restored and the stagnated function of the spleen (earth) may then be relieved. The spleen thereby restores the *kidney water* (water element) to help put out the *heart fire* or the *yang qi*. Finally the *heart fire* checks the excessive functions of the lung. This is an example of the mutual subjugation of the five *zang* organs.

The Relationship between
Yin-Yang and the *Five Elements*

The theories of *yin-yang* and the *five elements* were first recorded in the *Nei Jing*. Though different in their contexts, the theory of *yin-yang* complements that of the *five elements* in analyzing complex clinical problems. The theory of *yin-yang* is more fundamental. It establishes the complementary and oppositional nature of the two most basic elements applicable in TCM. The theory of the *five elements* is more specific and puts emphasis on illustrating the mutual relationship of various objects. Though far from being perfect, the limitations of these theories should be viewed in the light of the historical and experiential framework of TCM.

3

THE ORGANS

The theory of the organs in TCM relates anatomy, physiology and pathology together in the evaluation of the progression of disease. The theory uses anatomical and physiological terms (e.g. stomach, spleen, fluid, phlegm) similar to those used in Western medicine. However, the theory behind it and the anatomy referred to are very different from those currently used in Western medicine. In TCM it is believed that the organs are the core of the human body and are the centre for maintaining human life. If there is any imbalance or disease in the organs, TCM doctors should be able to observe this externally, quite unlike in Western medical practice. The theory of the organs attempts to explore the manifestation of disease and draw a clinical picture of what is happening in the viscera and organs in the body.

The *Zang-Fu* Organs

Zang-fu is a general term which stands for the five *solid* organs and the six *hollow* viscera of the human body.

The five *zang* organs refer to the heart, liver, spleen, lung and kidney, while the six *fu* organs comprise the gallbladder, stomach, small intestine, large intestine, bladder and the *sanjiao* (see subsequent sections of this chapter). It must be noted that these *zang-fu* organs may not always coincide with the anatomical organs. According to TCM, the *zang* organs store the essence and *qi* of the body and are functionally more important than the six *fu* organs which are responsible for absorption and assimilation.

In addition, there is the pericardium, which is the shield surrounding the heart. This has the function of protecting the heart against attack by external pathogenic factors and acts as a substitute for it in resisting injuries.

The Physiological Functions of the Five *Zang* Organs

Heart

The heart is the most important organ in the human body. The *Nei Jing* says, "The heart is the origin of life". As the key organ, it affects the health of the whole body. According to the theory of the organs, the heart houses the mind or mental faculties and it governs all the *zang-fu* organs, as well as the mental health and behaviour of people. The circulation of blood in the body is maintained by the heart, exactly as construed in Western medicine. The theory of the organs relates the heart to the tongue and draws an analogy that the tongue has a particular "tunnel vision" or orifice to the heart so that any pathology in the heart may be manifested on the tongue's surface. The tongue may look red or purple or may ulcerate at the tip when there is too much *heat* in the heart. A pale tongue denotes a deficiency in the heart.

Liver

The liver was compared to an army general by the ancient Chinese for its key role in warding off all external pathogens. The liver serves to store blood and regulates its distribution in the body. Blood stays in the liver when the body is at rest; but is also mobilized to the *zang-fu* organs, the channels and the meridians. Vomiting of blood is a result of a failure of the liver to store blood. Herbs which pacify the liver are frequently prescribed when the liver fails to store blood properly. In addition, the liver itself needs the nourishment of blood (which is *yin*) and deficiency in blood may result in an excess of *liver yang* or too much *heat* in the liver.

The liver also controls the tendons of the entire body and closely affects the movements of the limbs and joints. Seizure and opisthotonic contractions are regarded as pathology of the liver and tendon. As the tongue is related to the heart, the eye is considered to be the orifice to the liver. TCM ascribes acutely red and swollen eyes to too much *heat* in the liver and a chronic blurring of vision or dry eyes to a failure of the blood to properly nourish the liver. Treatment for such problems is therefore primarily targeted at the liver.

Spleen

The spleen is the organ responsible for digestion, absorption and nutrient assimilation in the human body. In the context of the *five elements*, the spleen is the organ pertaining to the earth. As long as the spleen is in good shape, the nutrients will be digested and distributed throughout the whole body. When the spleen malfunctions, the digestive process will be upset, giving rise to the symptoms of malnutrition, emaciation, loss of appetite, abdominal distension, diarrhea and kwashiorkor. The spleen also has the function of controlling and keeping the blood flowing within the blood vessels. Therefore, spleen-invigorating approaches are usually applied for patients who lose a great deal of blood, as in the case of chronic hemorrhage.

The spleen is also closely related to the muscles, the four limbs, the mouth and the lips. The mouth is the orifice to the spleen. Since the spleen governs the digestion and absorption of nutrients, a healthy spleen will maintain a good nutritional state in the body and strengthen the muscles and the four limbs; the lips would take on a healthy colour of red. If the spleen is in poor condition, however, the patient would have weakened muscles and would look pale.

Lung

The lung is in charge of *qi* and the respiration of the whole body. *Qi* (similar to *prana* in Indian philosophy) is in the air one inhales and in the food and water absorbed and transported to the lung. These two sources of *qi* are transformed in the lung into the so-called *genuine qi* (*zhen qi*). This *genuine qi* is regarded as the essential motive force of all functional activities of the human body, without which one would not be able to survive. The lung is closely related to the nose. Respiration takes place through the nose and thus it is held that the lung opens at the nose. The nose is frequently involved when the lung is affected. It is not uncommon for one to have a blocked nose when one coughs or is suffering from a respiratory tract infection. The lung is also associated with the skin surface. Those who have poor skin (i.e. a weak lung) sweat easily and are vulnerable to catching colds which may then be complicated by chest-related symptoms such as cough and shortness of breath. TCM, in addition, holds that the lung is the organ producing the voice. Hoarseness of voice, not surprisingly, is common in people with a common cold or a cough.

Kidney

The kidney stores two kinds of essence, the acquired and the congenital. The acquired essence is made up of the nutrients assimilated by the spleen to the kidney. Part of the essence is stored in the kidney in reserve for use while the rest is for bodily consumption. Congenital essence, inherited from one's parents, is inborn and is responsible for reproduction as well as for governing growth and the life processes from birth to old age. Even the bone and marrow are nourished by the kidney. Whether the bones are strong or not depends on the supply of nutrients from the kidney. Kyphosis complicating osteoporosis of the lumbar spine is ascribed to a deficiency of the kidney in supplying nutrients to the skeleton. Kidney-strengthening medicine is thus used for many ailments relating to the kidney.

The kidney also has a dual relationship with the brain as well as with the bone and marrow. In Chinese, the brain is called "the sea of marrow". This indirect cross-relation between the brain and marrow indicates the use of kidney-strengthening drugs to treat elderly patients suffering from senile dementia, dizziness and poor memory. In addition, the ears are the orifices to the two kidneys and the hair usually reflects the condition of the kidney. Patients with tinnitus or deafness due to a kidney deficiency have been treated effectively by administering the kidney-strengthening medicine.

Pericardium

The pericardium is the surrounding shield protecting the heart against direct exposure to diseases. TCM has traditionally viewed the heart as a monarch that should be guarded against external pathogenic factors. The pericardium and the heart are considered to perform approximately the same functions.

The Relations among the Five *Zang* Organs

The five *zang* organs are closely related to one another. Their mutual dependence, promoting and restraining one another, maintain the homeostasis of the bodily functions. As discussed in Chapter 2, the *zang* organs are ascribed to their respective *five elements*. The relationship between the *zang* organs may then be illustrated and studied using the theory of the *five elements*. Any excess or deficiency in an organ may therefore affect or be affected by its related element. An upset of the normal homeostasis of the bodily functions is the source of all diseases.

Although this concept of the *five elements* having a relationship with the organs is quite foreign to Westerners, it is a fundamental concept in TCM and must be accepted in order to gain an understanding of the whole science. Below are two examples that illustrate how the laws of mutual promotion and subjugation are applied in explaining the mechanism of disease and treatment. A hyperactive liver (wood) subdues the spleen (earth), upsets the normal functioning of the spleen and causes abdominal pain and diarrhea. Drugs acting on the liver (wood) and invigorating the spleen (earth) restore the normal wood-and-earth relationship for treatment. (See the table in Chapter 2.) In case of a spleen (earth) deficiency, the normal fluid balance would be lost and water retention would cause edema or diarrhea. Spleen-strengthening medicine and diuretics will therefore help the spleen to restore fluid assimilation.

The Physiological Functions of the Six *Fu* Organs

Gallbladder

The gallbladder stores the bile secreted by the liver to help digestion. Bile is considered in TCM to be the *qi* that has overflowed from the liver. Retention of bile causing jaundice is inevitable when the functioning of the gallbladder stagnates. Functionally the gallbladder is related to one's psychic state and personality. Panic, insomnia and psychiatric illnesses are often found to be related to the gallbladder.

Stomach

The stomach is described as "the sea of water and grains" in TCM for its continuous and voluminous accommodation of food and drink. Food is churned and partially digested in the stomach and is then passed over to the small intestine. The functioning of the stomach in TCM correlates exactly with Western medical concepts.

Small Intestine

The main function of the small intestine is to separate pure substances from waste. After preliminary digestion in the stomach, the food proceeds to the small intestine, where this separation takes place, again corresponding to the concepts in Western medicine. Pure substances refer to the absorbed essence of food, which nourishes the five *zang* organs and may be stored in the body. The waste is passed to the large intestine for disposal after the water is absorbed and sent to the bladder. Thus diseases of the small intestine may cause abnormal bowel and urinary symptoms.

Large Intestine

The large intestine is an organ of transportation. The waste not being absorbed by the small intestine is turned into faeces and discharged out of the body.

Bladder

The bladder controls urine excretion. It is a reservoir storing urine which is discharged when the bladder is full. Incontinence, for example, is due to a disease of the bladder. The balance of urine and the balance of other body fluids are closely related. Excessive loss of body fluids, such as in cases of profuse sweating, vomiting or diarrhea will decrease urine output. On the contrary, an increase in water intake or a decrease in water loss will expand the volume of body fluids and will increase urine ouput.

Sanjiao

The *sanjiao* (*san* means three, but *jiao* has no exact English equivalent) is a functional unit consisting of three portions, the upper *jiao* of the chest (heart and lung), the middle *jiao* of the upper abdomen (spleen and stomach) as well as the lower *jiao* of the lower abdomen (kidney and bladder). The *sanjiao* are not actually organs, but are three zones of the body within which various channels connect to govern the flow of nutrients and *qi* to that zone. The *sanjiao* have dual functions. They distribute and circulate *qi* and *blood*; and dredge the water passages so that excessive body fluids flow to the bladder for excretion.

The six *fu* organs coordinate together for the assimilation of food and body fluids. The stomach and the small and large intestines carry out the digestive functions and the transportation of food. The *sanjiao* and the small intestine assimilate water and body fluids and send them to the bladder. This understanding of the functions of the *fu* concurs remarkably with what we have learned from modern physiology.

The Interrelation between the Five *Zang* Organs and the Six *Fu* Organs

An affirmative coupling relation exists between the *zang* and *fu* organs. The liver is coupled to the gallbladder. The other pairs are heart and small intestine, spleen and stomach, lung and large intestine, kidney and bladder, as well as pericardium and *sanjiao*. A physiological upset or pathology in a *zang* organ will frequently involve its respective *fu* organ.

Relation between the Liver and the Gallbladder

The gallbladder is attached to the liver. It receives bile or *qi* from the liver. The function of the two organs are so closely related that there is no need to emphasize their difference in TCM. In fact it is sometimes difficult to decide which to look at when certain symptoms appear, such as chills or fever, a fullness in the chest, a bitter taste in the mouth or vomiting. These symptoms are seen as being caused by too much *heat* in the liver and the gallbladder meridians. Drugs acting on the liver are often interchangeable with those acting on the gallbladder. Thus liver-pacifying herbs can also be used to reduce *heat* in the gallbladder, and vice versa.

Relation between the Spleen and the Stomach

The stomach churns and digests food while the spleen assimilates the essence of food and sends it to different parts of the body. Neither one alone may accomplish the complete nutritional supply to the body. The bonding between the two organs is so strong that when one is diseased, the other is also involved. When the stomach fails to accommodate food or when one is anorexic, the spleen will not be able to transport the nutrients efficiently. If the spleen is mal-functioning, the stomach will fail to accommodate the food, resulting in either vomiting or diarrhea.

Relation between the Heart and the Small Intestine

Diseases of the heart often affect the small intestine. Symptoms of having too much *heat* in the heart, such as tongue ulcers, are often complicated with symptoms of excessive *heat* in the small intestine, for example a decrease in urine output. Treatment in TCM is to dissipate excessive *heat* in both the heart and the small intestine and increase urine output so that the *heat* in excess may be expelled through urination.

Relation between the Lung and the Large Intestine

Lung diseases may affect the large intestine. For example, too much *heat* in the lung may cause constipation. Treating the large intestine may conversely relieve lung symptoms. Purgatives which promote the free flow of *qi* in the lung are useful for patients who have problems like phlegm retention.

Relation between the Kidney and the Bladder

Body fluids are converted to urine by the *qi* of the kidney before it can be passed into the bladder for excretion. When there is difficulty in these functions, the *qi* of the kidney and bladder has to be treated with a warming remedy in order to restore its normal function of urine formation.

Relation between the Pericardium and the Sanjiao

The *sanjiao* is the outward guard of the *zang-fu* organs while the pericardium is the outward guard of the heart. Their close relation reinforces their protective functions of the main viscera of the body.

The Extraordinary *Fu* Organs

In addition to the five *zang* and six *fu* organs, there are *extraordinary fu* organs, also called "peculiar *hollow*" organs, although in Western medicine these would not all be considered independent organs. Their main function is to store the essence of life. They are the brain, marrow, bones, blood vessels, gallbladder and uterus. The gallbladder is the same as that of the six *fu* organs. The bones, brain and marrow have already been mentioned in the section on the kidney. The blood vessels are under the control of the heart. They store blood and circulate it to the whole body.

The uterus is the organ for menstruation and it accommodates the fetus. The physiology of menstruation has been described in the *Nei Jing* in detail. It was recorded that menstruation is a monthly phenomenon in girls starting at the age of 14 and stopping at the age of 49. This corresponds with Western understanding of menstruation, but exactly how it works is seen quite differently. According to TCM, in the teens, the *kidney qi* is vigorous to encourage growth and development. At the age of around 14, the amount of *qi* is abundant enough to open up the channels between the uterus and the two particular meridians, called *Chong* and *Ren*. The blood is then able to feed the uterus. Menstruation is regarded as an overflow of blood in the uterus. It takes another month for the empty *Chong* and *Ren* meridians to be filled up with blood again before another cycle of menstruation begins again. This process will continue until the female reaches the age of around 49 when the *kidney qi* and *blood* become exhausted. The *Chong* and *Ren* meridians collapse and then menstruation ceases.

A Comparison of the Views of TCM and Western Medicine on the Five *Zang* Organs

Both TCM and Western medicine share the same terminology for the viscerae or the *zang* organs (heart, liver, spleen, lung and kidney). However the concepts of the viscera referred to are not exactly identical. The pancreas is not recognized as a viscera or *zang* organ in TCM. These conceptual differences may be attributed to the diverse historical development of medicine in China and the West. Dissection and autopsy are not acceptable to the majority of people in China, thus discouraging anatomical study of the human body. By and large, the theories of TCM have been derived from careful observations of the external manifestations of diseases without referring to the individual viscera.

Different patterns of disease manifestations are classified into syndromes pertaining to the five *zang* and six *fu* organs.

The *zang-fu* organs, as mentioned before, are considered to be independent, yet inter-related functional subordinates of a unified entity. On the other hand, Western medicine, through dissection and autopsy, has a more thorough understanding of human anatomy and describes in detail the location, morphology and size of a viscera. With advancing technology, we know that the physiology and anatomy of an organ extends to the cellular and subcellular level. The observation of organs in Western medicine is based essentially on the morphological structures, and changes in the organ's physiological and biochemical functions, rather than the manifestation of symptoms as in TCM.

A comparison of TCM and Western medicine with respect to the five *zang* organs is summarized below.

The Heart

The *zang* theory that "the heart controls the blood circulation" is in line with the Western concept of the circulation-maintaining function of the organ. However, in TCM, unlike in Western medicine, the functions of the heart go beyond mere circulatory pumping. Chinese medicine states that the heart has a similar function as the brain in affecting one's emotional state, thinking and other mental activities. If the heart is diseased, the brain's functions may also be deranged, giving rise to symptoms ranging from sleeping disorders and hypochondria to psychosis and coma.

The Liver

TCM holds that the liver is located at both of the hypochondria rather than on present-day understanding of the site of the liver being at the right hypochondrium. Pain, fullness and distending pain at the hypochondrium are seen as being caused by the stagnation of the *liver qi*. In fact, a pathology along the liver meridian, which runs for example along the genitals, both sides of the lower abdomen, the hypochondriac regions and the nipples, is regarded as a sign of stagnation of the *liver qi*. In other words, what is wrong in the liver often is not due to a poorly-functioning liver or liver failure. Certainly these concepts are out of context with what is described as the liver in Western medicine.

The Spleen

The spleen is located at the left hypochondrium. A person can still survive after splenectomy, which means that this viscus is not indispensable. The understanding of the spleen is entirely different in TCM from Western medicine. The spleen is life-supporting and is responsible for digestion as well as the assimilation of nutrients and body fluids for the whole body. A sick spleen results in indigestion and malabsorption, which can cause abdominal distension, edema and loose stool. According to Western medicine, these are symptoms of the digestive system involving the gut and pancreas rather than the spleen. The spleen is also the site where phlegm is produced. In TCM terms, "the lung stores the phlegm, and the phlegm originates from the spleen". Patients suffering from chronic bronchitis produce a substantial amount of phlegm. But according to Western medicine, the increased sputum production is due to hyperactive mucus glands in the bronchus. This illustrates that the spleen in TCM is very different from the spleen which we understand in modern physiology and anatomy.

The Lung

In TCM, the lung controls *qi* and is the organ for respiration. It cleanses the inhaled air and directs the air and *qi* downwards. This implies that the lung is able to eliminate external pathogens. Failing to do so, the *lung qi* would ascend rather than descend, thus giving rise to respiratory problems. Once the external pathogenic factors are eliminated and the phlegm is cleared with drugs, the *zang* function of the lung sending the *qi* downwards is restored and the respiratory symptoms will be resolved. This concept of the lung basically corresponds to the functioning of the respiratory system of Western medicine, but without reference to *qi*.

The TCM teaching of "the *lung* dominates the skin and hair" suggests that the lung's actions coordinate with the skin and sweat glands. When *lung qi* is weak, the patient will be susceptible to respiratory tract infections and is apt to perspire. The pores of the skin are known as the "doors of the *qi*", meaning that they serve as outlets for the drainage of *qi*. Thus problems of the lung can often be seen on the skin and hair, a concept not recognized in Western medicine.

The Kidney

While the *spleen* is the key organ that acquires nutrients, the kidney is the source of one's inborn constitution. This inborn essence is the element affecting the whole process of growth, development and ageing, depending on the amount of *kidney qi* in the body. The cycle of growth and death runs parallel with the escalation and decline of *qi*.

Thus the part the kidney plays in the ageing process is an important one. As discussed earlier, the kidney is closely related to the ears and hair. There is also a well-known saying in TCM: "The kidney controls the bones and the teeth are an extension of the bones." All this implies that certain geriatric problems such as low back pain, osteoporotic bone pain, greying of hair, tinnitus and otosclerosis, and loss of teeth are associated with kidney deficiency. TCM also puts the blame of impotence and spontaneous emission of semen on kidney deficiency.

The most significant similarity between TCM and Western medicine concerning the kidney is its role in the regulation of body fluids. In both TCM and Western medicine, many ailments such as edema are seen to have their origin in the kidneys.

From what we have so far discussed, there seem to be more differences than similarities between TCM and Western medicine regarding the understanding of the viscera or *zang-fu* organs. Despite unmatching anatomical descriptions, both schools share some common points of view on the physiology of the body. Both parties recognize the role of the heart in maintaining blood circulation, the intestine in digestion and absorption, the lung in respiration as well as the kidney in the balance of fluids and urination. However, the descriptions of the spleen have virtually nothing in common.

What has been discussed is only a preliminary understanding of the theories in TCM with reference to the physiology and anatomy of Western medicine. Further research is warranted to explore a new approach towards treatment using the best of both TCM and Western medicine.

4

QI, BLOOD AND BODY FLUIDS

Qi, blood and body fluids are regarded as the basic compositions of the body by which the *zang-fu* organs, channels, tissues and viscera function. *Qi* is dynamic, active and invisible. It activates and warms the body and is thus ascribed to the *yang* category. Blood, in TCM terminology, is not very different from the understanding of Western medicine. Body fluids is a generic term for all kinds of fluids in the body. Both blood and body fluids have nourishing and moistening functions. Thus they belong to the *yin* category. The natural history of a disease and development of the human body from birth to death are closely affected by the flows and changes of *qi*, blood and body fluids

Qi

Qi is the motive force promoting the physiological activities of all the *zang-fu* organs. There are two types of *qi* in the body. *Congenital qi* begins at birth and is inherited from one's parents. This energy originates from the kidneys and is stored in the *"dantian"*, a place three *cuns* (Chinese inches) below the navel. The other type of *qi* is acquired after birth. This is the *acquired qi* that we get from food and water, which is assimilated by the spleen and stomach, and from the air inhaled by the lungs. The *acquired qi* is constantly replenished, and is a fundamental substance maintaining the life activities of the human body. It is said that "human life is completely dependent upon this kind of *qi*". Both types of *qi* work together, circulating in the body along the channels and nourishing the body. *Qi* is capable of producing and controlling blood, warming and nourishing the tissues, building up resistance against diseases as well as activating the physiological functions of the *zang-fu* organs. *Qi* is function-specific and carries different names according to the role it plays or the *zang-fu* organ it serves. The characteristics of various types of *qi* are discussed as below.

Pectoral Qi

This is the *qi* in the chest and exhaled through the throat. When it descends, it coordinates with the heart to promote blood circulation. Thus the *pectoral qi* is associated with both respiration and circulation. The volume of one's voice, respiration, the circulation of *qi* and blood, and the warmth or coldness of the limbs are all related to the activity of *pectoral qi*.

Qi of the Zang-fu Organs

This *qi* in the five *zang* and six *fu* organs is often called *genuine qi*. It is essential for the *zang-fu* organs to carry out their functions. In the spleen, it is called the *spleen qi*. In the lung, it is called the *lung qi*. By means of the respective types of *qi*, the spleen is able to digest, transform and absorb nutrients; the stomach can accommodate food for digestion; the lung performs respiration and the kidney enables the human body to grow.

Nutrient Qi

The *nutrient qi* transforms into blood in the vessels. It circulates together with blood to nourish the whole body. Its basic functions are identical to blood. Therefore both blood and *nutrient qi* are often referred to at the same time.

Protective Qi

The *protective qi* is part of the *yang qi* in the body. It circulates outside the blood vessels, spreading all over the body, and serves to warm and nourish the *zang-fu* organs and muscles. Externally, the *qi* moistens the skin and controls the perspiration and intactness of the skin. Causes of disease are thus kept away from the body by the *protective qi*.

Qi is moving constantly within the human body with definite circulating directions and rules. The *lung qi* descends while the *stomach qi* and the *spleen qi* ascend. Travelling against the proper direction may induce a physiological upset of the respective *zang-fu* organs. Adverse ascending of *lung qi* may cause coughing and asthma. Similarly, nausea and vomiting occur whenever the *stomach qi* ascends.

Qi becomes stagnant when its circulation is interrupted. Distending discomfort or pain, which is often fleeting, may be noted in the involved areas.

Blood

In TCM, blood is said to come from the essence of food and water, after being digested and assimilated by the stomach and the spleen and transformed by the heart and lung. The blood, propelled by the heart and *yang qi*, circulates to nourish the *zang-fu* organs, skin, muscles, tendons and bones. The *spleen qi* controls the blood and keeps it within the blood vessels. In TCM, we also have the concept of "the liver storing the blood". This can be illustrated by the quote, "Blood flows into the vessels when one lies down, and stays in the liver when one is at rest".

It is understood that the flow of blood and *qi* in the meridians and vessels is interdependent. However, nobody in TCM questions the fact that the key propelling factor is the *qi*. We quote, "*qi* commands the blood". If the flow of *qi* is interfered with, then the flow of blood will stagnate. *Qi* not only pushes blood circulation, but also helps to recycle the blood through its breakdown and regeneration. Massive bleeding results in an exhaustion of *qi*. If this vicious circle is uninterrupted, a deficiency of both *qi* and blood would be inevitable.

Body Fluids

Body fluid is a generic term for all kinds of fluids in the body. It comprises major fluids circulating in the body as well as various kinds of secretions such as sweat, saliva, stomach secretions, intestinal secretions and urine.

The formation, distribution and excretion of body fluids is a comparatively complex physiological process involving the lung, spleen, kidney, stomach, small intestine, large intestine and urinary bladder. The fluids within the body originate from the water coming into the stomach with food and drink. The fluid in the stomach is sent upwards to the lung and then distributed to the other *zang-fu* organs, such as the spleen. While part of the fluid in the lung is vaporized and exhaled, the rest is directed downwards to the kidney where excessive water and wastes in the fluid are extracted from the *qi* and then stored in the urinary bladder for excretion as urine.

The chief functions of the body fluids are: (1) to nourish the internal organs, skin, mucous membrane and muscles; (2) to lubricate the joints and provide substrate for the secretory glands and tears; and (3) to transform into sweat and urine and then to be excreted with the waste.

In summary, the turnover of the body fluids is a complex process comprising the stomach's accommodation, the spleen's digestion and assimilation, the lung's distribution and the kidney's coordination. The role of the kidney is probably the most important. It is the *kidney qi* which nourishes and activates the physiological function of the other *zang-fu* organs. The *qi* also controls the formation and excretion of urine. The kidney is so important in fluid metabolism that it is called the "*zang* organ of water", since it is in charge of the body fluids of the whole body. The organs participating in fluid control are grouped as the *sanjiao* (see Chapter 3, page 30).

APPENDIX:
Modern Interpretation of the
"Blood Stasis" Syndrome

From a physiological point of view, stagnant blood flow may cause blood congestion. This occurs in congestive heart failure, portal hypertension and thrombophlebitis. Blood stasis due to hemorrhage, ecchymosis and hematoma formation may also be classified as stagnation of blood. Based on this concept, TCM regards all swellings or tumors as blood stasis. Some of the symptoms of blood stasis in TCM are manifestations of stagnant blood flow: cyanotic tongue, congested and dilated veins, varicose vein and caput medusa in the abdomen. Tenderness and pain sensation are also regarded as physical signs of blood stasis. Clinical examples are appendicitis, hepatitis, perforated peptic ulcer and ectopic pregnancy. Visceromegaly, tumour, swelling, hemorrhagic signs such as tarry stool in bleeding peptic ulcer, petechiae, purpura and hemorrhagic symptoms of epistaxis, and menorrhagia, all are evidences of blood stasis as well. Other miscellaneous conditions of blood stasis are menopause, amenorrhea, eclampsia, psoriasis, scleroderma, paralysis, paresthesia or sensory loss, ascites, edema, alopecia, hyperpigmentation, amnesia and mania.

Patients with blood stasis may have abnormal laboratory test results. Their blood or plasma viscosity is higher than normal. They may also have a high packed cell volume, blood fibrinogen content and increased erythrocyte sedimentation rate. The red cell electrophoretic time, which is a measure of electric charge on the erythrocyte, is also higher in patients with blood stasis. The red cells and platelets are more liable to aggregate and the thrombolytic activity is decreased. When the viscosity is high, the blood tends to coagulate, often leading to thrombosis in the blood vessels.

The microcirculation system often is not normal in patients suffering from blood stasis. Microangiopathy such as abnormal capillary proliferation as well as increase in arteriolar spasm, stenosis and deformity may be detectable. These interfere with the free flow of red cells in the microcirculation. The capillary may become permeable and fragile. Exudates and microhemorrhages with or without thrombosis may be present.

Blood stasis, whenever it appears, should be relieved and removed by herbs which promote circulation. Red sage root, compound red sage root (red sage root, Dalbergia wood), Rhizoma Ligustici Safflower, Radix Paeoniae Rubra, peach kernel, and motherwort reduce blood viscosity and platelet aggravation, restore normal blood flow and improve tissue hypoxia. Thus microcirculation disturbance may be alleviated. Blood stasis is an important field for research on integrative therapy of TCM and modern medicine. Preliminary research has shown more and more diseases being responsive to this form of anti-stasis treatment. Encouraging results have appeared in the treatment of coronary heart disease, hepatitis, nephritis, rheumatoid arthritis, diabetes, apoplexy, epilepsy, dysfunctional uterine bleeding, epistaxis, nerve deafness, psoriasis and anaphylactoid purpura. The new treatment protocol also lowers operation rate in surgical diseases such as endometriosis and thromboangiitis obliterans. Clinical control of chronic and persistent diseases such as systemic lupus erythematosus, scleroderma, and liver cirrhosis has also been reported. The mortality rate and relapse rate of myocardial infarction may be reduced through the therapy which promotes blood circulation and eliminates blood stasis.

5

CAUSES OF DISEASE

TCM classifies all causes of disease, known as pathogens, into exogenous and endogenous factors. The former is due to insults from outside the body while the latter is derived from deranged functions of the internal organs. The rationale of this classification is inspired by the Chinese cognition of the close relation between man and nature and that people cannot escape the influences of nature. When there is a weather change concomitant with a deficiency of *genuine qi*, the resistance of a person might be too low to fight against disease. Other than these environmental factors, sharp and blunt injuries, insect bites and trauma are also considered to be exogenous factors.

Emotional changes are inevitable in daily life. One's psyche and emotional upset are also related to diseases. Extreme joy, anger, melancholy or happiness may cause diseases. Abnormal patterns in diet, sexual activity and overwork are also considered to be endogenous factors. The concept that a dramatic change in weather can cause illness is widely accepted in the West, but the idea that one's emotions can also cause illness is quite new. Nevertheless, common sense tells us that the way we live has a direct effect on our health.

Exogenous Factors

The Six Abnormal Climatic Factors

Man is subject to all sorts of changes in nature. In most places the weather changes according to the four seasons in a cycle of spring warmness, summer heat, autumn cool and winter cold. In between seasons, severe weather changes are not uncommon. Witnessing various phenomena like tornados, rain, mist, dew, frost, snow, cloudy and sunny weather, and dry spells, it was hypothesized that these changes were caused by the constant movement of the six climatic factors of *wind, cold, summer heat, dampness, dryness* and *fire*. The normal functions of the six kinds of climate are as follows:

1. *Dryness* serves to make things dry;
2. *Summer* heat vaporizes water;
3. *Wind* stirs and blows everything;
4. *Dampness* moistens all;
5. *Cold* hardens all sorts of things; and
6. *Fire* warms everything.

Environmental changes within a certain limit are not in themselves harmful. However, any drastic change in the six climatic factors may have an adverse influence on people. Unexpected changes such as cold temperature in spring, hot weather in autumn or chilly cold in autumn may be encountered. Abnormal weather is detrimental to all living creatures and can cause illness in people. The six climatic factors are thus considered to be major exogenous pathogenic factors and are called six abnormal climatic factors in TCM.

1. *Wind*: This is regarded as the most important pathogenic factor. It is characterized by the characteristic

windy properties of being ever-changing, wandering, difficult to catch as well as being sudden in onset and withdrawal. *Wind* may cause a wide variety of diseases. The *Nei Jing* says, "*Wind* is the first and foremost factor in causing various diseases". The changes of *wind* in the climate have long been recognized to be very important in inducing disease.

Wind, being pathogenic in itself, may catalyze the other five abnormal climatic factors in attacking the health. With *cold*, it is called *wind-cold*; with *dampness*, it is called *wind-dampness*; with *fire*, it is called *wind-fire*. In view of its characteristics, *wind* may induce the other five abnormal climatic factors to attack the human body. Clinical manifestations and signs of these diseases may be as variable as or change as quickly as *wind*. *Wind* per se may cause symptoms such as fever, sweating and headaches. In the presence of other climatic factors, additional symptoms may occur. Chills, myalgia and bone pain may be reported in cases of *wind-cold*. A combination of *wind-heat* may give rise to *heat* symptoms of dryness of mouth, irritability, deep-red urine and constipation. *Wind-fire* may cause red eyes and a sore throat. Careful differentiation of the clinical patterns is essential to avoid confusion of the intricate and ever-changing manifestations of disease.

2. *Cold*: Cold air can attack the human body continually throughout the year, especially in winter. The symptoms caused by pathogenic *cold* are fever, inability to sweat, headaches, myalgia, back pain and arthralgia. Physical examination may show a superficial and tense pulse as well as a thin white tongue coating. If the *cold* invades deep into the spleen and stomach, there may be diarrhea and abdominal

pain which can be relieved by *heat*. The pulse will become deep and slow while the tongue will be white.

3. *Summer heat*: Diseases caused by *summer heat* occur most frequently in summer, particularly during a hot summer. There are two different types of manifestation. The major one is *yang heat* accompanied by headache, high fever, thirst, irritability and sweating. The other kind of *summer heat* symptoms are of the *yin* type. These occur when people expose themselves to the cold at night, sleeping in the open and having too many cold drinks. These patients may complain of cold, headache, giddiness, abdominal pain, vomiting, diarrhea, fullness in the chest and loss of appetite.

4. *Dampness*: Too much humidity in the air or what TCM calls *pathogenic damp* is detrimental to health. In China, June is the most humid and rainy month. June is called the late summer season in TCM. In this humid season, diseases may be contracted when one is exposed to dew and fog in the air, sweat and wet clothes or even when one sits on the damp ground or works in the water. Symptoms caused by *dampness* include tiredness and heaviness of the body, lassitude, edema, painful joints, chest discomfort, nausea, abdominal distension, loss of appetite, jaundice and diarrhea.

5. *Dryness*: It is usually dry in autumn. Extreme dryness is not good for health and may cause disease. There may be a loss of body fluids, resulting in symptoms characterized by diseases of the *dry* type. The results are a sore and dry throat, an unproductive cough, thick sputum, a dry mouth, frequent thirst and constipation.

6. *Fire*: The concept of *fire* is similar to that of *heat*. It is an extreme of the *heat* manifestation. However, *fire* has its own characteristics different from those of *heat*. The

latter usually causes diseases in summer when the weather is hot. However, the scope of *fire* covers a much wider area. In addition to *heat,* other exogenous factors, i.e. *wind, cold, summer heat, dampness and dryness,* may be involved in causing an illness. When these factors reach a more serious stage, symptoms may emerge through the intermediate stage where *heat* turns into *fire.* At this stage, *fire* symptoms include convulsion, coma, delirium, a dry mouth and cracked lips, a flushed face, profuse sweating and a high fever. *Fire* symptoms come from a derangement of the different kinds of *qi.* The *fire* in the body consumes a large amount of body fluids, aggravating the symptoms and thus pushing the disease to a more critical stage.

Epidemics

The epidemic factor is another pathogen. Its origin is thought to come from abnormal changes in weather along with the fermentation of dirty and stale products. It is more likely to occur at times of turmoil and the chaos of war, when sanitary conditions are at their worst. The spread of disease may be very fast and the symptoms are acute in their onset. Owing to cross infection, the manifestation of the disease is predictable. This understanding of epidemics is compatible with infectious diseases we know of today. It is believed the disease is acquired by the inhalation of epidemic factors through the mouth and nose.

Traumatic Injuries

Traumatic injuries may be sustained by sharp and blunt objects, accidents like slipping and falling as well as insect or animal bites. Wounds inflicted by knives, weapons or falls may cause local injury, swelling, pain, bleeding and soft tissue or bone injuries. Resulting diseases due to injuries may be life threatening. Insect and animal bites not only cause direct superficial wounds, but also invite exposure to noxious venoms and poisons, jeopardizing the body's health.

Parasites

Parasitic diseases have been known in TCM for a very long time. In TCM, schistosoma is called the "water poison" or the "venomous worm". Malaria prevalent in mountainous areas is called a "pestilential pathogen". Intestinal infestation of parasites was also well documented a long time ago in TCM. The ascaris and pinworm are described as the "long worm" and "short white worm" respectively. Taenia has also been documented as a parasite in the gut treatable with betel nut. Fruit of the Rangoon creeper was used to treat ascariasis. Their clinical effectiveness has been well recognized and they remain in use today.

Endogenous Factors

The Seven Emotional Factors

The seven emotional factors is a term which covers the range of emotions of joy, anger, melancholy, anxiety, grief, fear and fright. Emotional factors, being taken as part of the main causes of disease, constitute a specific component of TCM theory. Emotional activities are said to be closely related to the occurrence of diseases. Hardly anyone can be exempt from emotional changes when dealing with other people or with their particular surroundings. Ups and downs in emotions are inevitable. Emotional change within a normal range is not harmful to the human body. Only when the variations go beyond a limit or the stress becomes too great would the normal functioning of the *zang-fu* organs be affected. Emotional changes are looked upon as endogenous in origin.

1. *Joy*: Joy and laughter are the emotions of happiness. Usually joy is not pathogenic. However, extreme emotion due to joy consumes the *qi* excessively and impairs the functioning of the heart. The *Nei Jing* says, "The *heart qi* is damaged when there is too much joy or laughter." It is a common experience to feel exhausted after laughing for too long. There is an old Chinese proverb, "Extreme joy begets sorrow". This is quite compatible with the TCM theory.

2. *Anger*: As pointed out earlier in Chapter 3, great anger injures the liver. To carry it further, the *Nei Jing* pointed out that extreme anger may result in syncope. When anger is expressed, one often notes a pale complexion, tremor in the limbs and fainting attacks. Even a slight element of anger may upset one's appetite. Hence anger is considered one of the endogenous pathogenic factors that may affect the human body.

3. *Melancholy*: Melancholy is an emotion which involves the feelings of depression and despair. Ill health is expected if the melancholic feeling persists for a long time. It is a common experience that anorexia and inability to taste often coexist with feeling bad. According to the *zang-fu* theory, anorexia is a manifestation of the poor functioning of the spleen and stomach due to melancholy.

4. *Anxiety*: A pathological anxious state due to various causes shows symptoms of dizziness, eye strain, insomnia, amnesia and palpitation.

5. *Grief*: Grief is a sentimental emotion and a mental agony. Grief may damage the *zang-fu* organs of the heart and lung and thus cause illnesses. An example is somebody falling unconscious upon hearing of a loved one's death.

6. *Fear*: Fear is also a mental stress. It is endogenous in origin and is often related to being too tense. The strain, if beyond being acceptable, may damage both the heart and the kidney according to TCM theory.

7. *Fright*: Fright is somewhat different from fear. The former is a reaction to an exogenous noxious stimulation such as a mishap or a loud noise, whereas the latter comes entirely from within. As a reaction to something unforeseeable, fright is not predictable. Symptoms of fright are a phobia of noise, nightmares, sudden waking and shrieking in sleep. Children may have nocturnal fevers and mental sluggishness.

Abnormal Diet

The effect of diet on health has been understood in TCM for a long time. Obsessive, unhygienic or careless eating habits may damage the *zang-fu* organs. Both the spleen and stomach may be affected. When the digestive and assimilative functions are affected, disease may occur as a complication. In China, there is an old saying warning about the importance of diet related to health: "Illness often finds its way in through the mouth".

Intemperance in Sexual Activities

It is well-recognized in TCM that overindulgence in sexual activity can damage the kidney. As the kidney stores the *congenital qi*, kidney deficiency as a result of sexual intemperance may give rise to vertigo, dizziness, night sweats, palpitation, leg weakness, low back pain, lassitude, malaise, and involuntary seminal ejaculation. Excessive sexual activity is discouraged in TCM.

Overfatigue

Working takes up an important share of our time in daily life. Normal work activity not only is not detrimental to health, but enhances the circulation of *qi* and *blood* and thus is of benefit to one's health. However, overstrain or over-exertion without appropriate relaxation demolishes the *qi* in the middle *jiao*. Diseases with symptoms of shortness of breath, lassitude, a feeble voice with shallow breath, fatigue, and anorexia may be acquired. TCM warns that "overwork exhausts the *qi*" and stresses the importance of balancing one's workload with appropriate relaxation.

Phlegm and Blood Stasis

Phlegm and blood stasis are two other pathogenic factors which may either cause diseases or aggravate their severity. Phlegm is formed whenever there is excessive production of fluid or a stagnation in the flow of *qi* in the *zang-fu* organs. As an organ responsible for fluid assimilation, the spleen, of all the *zang-fu* organs, contributes most to the production of phlegm. The accumulation of phlegm causes a variety of symptoms according to the location of pathology. Palpitation, disorientation and psychosis are the manifestations when the heart is involved. Phlegm in the stomach causes nausea and anorexia. When the head is involved, dizziness, vertigo, nausea and vomiting may result. Lymph node enlargement, goitre and subcutaneous nodules are also regarded as the result of the stagnation of phlegm underneath the skin and along the meridians.

Blood stasis denotes either stagnation of blood flow in the circulation or in a local area, or an accumulation of blood forming an ecchymosis. It may find expression in persistent pain, hepatomegaly, splenomegaly, ecchymosis, purpura, shallow skin complexion, cyanosis of the tongue and lips, dysmenorrhea, postpartum bleeding.

According to TCM, illnesses are due to either exogenous or endogenous pathogens. This understanding, as mentioned earlier, appears to be crude compared with the more complex modern explanation of disease mechanisms. In fact, the etiological theory of TCM is indeed very different from that of modern medicine. However, the concepts in TCM were put forward more than two thousand years ago when scientific instruments and technology were not sophisticated enough to explore etiological factors such as bacteria and viruses. Yet this philosophy still plays an important role in guiding the diagnosis and treatment of illnesses in the practice of TCM. The etiological theory deserves study for its practical value. It tells us of the relation between nature and the human body as well as the importance of emotional factors, diet and lifestyle. The theory also educates us on how to keep fit and strong. It cautions us to watch out for and adapt to weather changes. We are urged to be optimistic and happy in mood. Rules for diet and living are offered for prevention of disease. This legacy of our ancient teachings merits attention and further promotion.

6

METHODS OF DIAGNOSIS AND DIFFERENTIATION OF SYNDROMES

TCM has a unique approach to diagnosis, quite different from Western medicine. Clinical information collected after completing the four diagnostic procedures of inspection, listening and smelling, inquiring, and palpation are analyzed according to eight principles of TCM as well as other TCM theories (found later in this chapter) before deciding on the clinical approach to the patient's problems.

The Four Diagnostic Methods

Inspection

This is a diagnostic method by which the doctor observes the patient's vitality, colour and general appearance in order to gain a first-hand initial impression. Inspection is probably the most important *a priori* procedure in TCM practice. Below are the four main considerations.

1. *Vitality*:

   The colour, complexion and lustre of the skin and the overall general impression of the patient are the key points in observation. The complexion is an excellent indicator of the vitality of the human body. An active and happy appearance suggests that a person possesses strong bodily resistance and a good prognosis is to be expected. On the contrary, if a patient appears to be apathetic and stuporous, the prognosis is guarded, even though the illness is not quite serious. The general impression given by a patient is difficult to define in words. The recognition of patterns in the health status of a subject can only be acquired through years of experience. Anything that appears to be abnormal or deviates from the normal physical signs is considered abnormal. The skin and colour of one's complexion may reveal problems in the vital functions of the *zang-fu* organs. The five colours (blue-green, yellow, red, white/pale and black/dark) may reflect the conditions of the corresponding five *zang* organs (heart, liver, spleen, lung and kidney). Thus a blue-green colour implies that the liver is sick. The lustre of one's colour is equally important. Moist and bright lustres indicate a good prognosis whereas dry and dim lustres suggest the contrary.

2. *Body Appearance*:

   Much can be learned from the appearance of the body. It is difficult for *yang qi* to be distributed in a fat body. Owing to stagnation of the *phlegm*, a fat person is liable to cerebrovascular attacks or strokes. This diagnosis is very similar to a Western doctor's.

However the concept of why an overweight person might be susceptible to these diseases is completely different. A thin subject with a small build has a deficiency of *yin blood*. The imbalance of *yin* and *yang* gives rise to hyperactivity of *deficiency fire*, thus various related symptoms may emerge. Those who put on a lot of clothes in summer usually suffer from diseases categorized as being of a *cold* nature while those who dress lightly in winter are more likely to contract diseases of a *heat* nature. Such information is noteworthy for reference in the clinical management in TCM.

3. *Facial Features*:
   The facial expression can tell a doctor about the psychological status of a patient, whether he or she is anxious, melancholic, happy or elated. Any element of endogenous pathogenic factors as mentioned in Chapter 5 should be considered and referred to when writing the prescription for the patient. In the inspection of the eye, a redness usually denotes a *heat* syndrome while clear eyes denote a *cold* syndrome. Dry eyes are related to the presence of *dry heat*. A yellowish discoloration of the eyes shows an occurrence of *damp heat* and is an early sign of jaundice of the body. A stuffy nose with turbid nasal discharge suggests that the cause of the disease is the exogenous pathogen of *wind heat*. *Wind cold*, on the contrary, brings a clear discharge to the blocked nostrils. The clearness or turbidity of the nasal discharge helps to distinguish between *cold* and *heat*. In acute diseases, a flaring of the nostrils is an evidence of retention of *excess heat* in the lung. However, the same symptom in chronic diseases suggests that there is a deficiency of the lung in the patient and implies a critical state of the illness.

Redness and swelling of the mouth and lips indicate *extreme heat*. Burning red lips concur with a *yin deficiency* which results in hyperactivity of the *fire*. Thus *deficiency* and *excess* may thereby be differentiated according to the *yin-yang* theory. Deviation of the angle of the mouth is evidence of a stroke or facial palsy, while tight clenching of the jaws when not speaking suggests a seizure or neurological involvement.

4.   *The Tongue and Its Coating*:
Tongue inpection is a vital diagnostic procedure in TCM. Although Western doctors do check a patient's tongue in certain cases, tongue inspection in the West is far less complex and important than in Chinese medicine. In TCM, both the tongue coating and the tongue itself have to be studied. The tongue, or the body of the tongue, manifests the *vital qi* in the human body, as well as the status of *deficiency* and *excess* of the five *zang* organs. The tongue coating reflects the involvement of the six exogenous pathogenic factors in a patient. It grows on the tongue like grass growing on the surface of soil. The spleen and the stomach act like the soil which nourishes the tongue coating. The normal coating is thin and moist. If a patient is invaded by exogenous pathogens, the coating grows thick, as in the case of an uncontrolled growth of grass. In the case of a *vital qi* deficiency, the assimilation function of the spleen and stomach would be weakened and would be insufficient to nourish the body. The tongue surface thus appears to be smooth like a mirror and is covered with a very thin coating. According to TCM theory, all the five *zang* organs receive *qi* from the stomach. The appearance of the tongue may reflect the functions of the *zang* organs through the interaction of *stomach qi* with the other *zang-fu* organs.

The tongue can be in various colours, according to the state of the patient. A normal tongue is moist and has an appropriate red colour. A light red or pale tongue is a sign of a deficiency of both *qi* and *blood*. A bright red tongue shows the presence of *heat*, and usually indicates a *yin deficiency*. A deep red tongue shows that the disease has already penetrated into the *yin* system. A thick, purplish tongue is often associated with alcoholism, and a bluish tongue indicates an extreme deficiency of *blood* and *qi*, and is evidence of a critical illness. All this of course is only a general description; actual diagnosis involves a much deeper understanding of the different states of the tongue and how they relate to indications of disease.

Another factor which must be considered in observing the patient's tongue is the colour of the coating of the tongue. A normal tongue coating is generally thin and white. The root of the tongue often has a layer of sticky coating. If there is too much *cold* in the stomach, an accumulation of *phlegm* in the body will occur and will be reflected by a thick and sticky coating on the tongue. The tongue of a cigarette smoker is often yellow. In addition, a yellow tongue coating may be found in *interior* syndromes due to exogenous pathogenic factors. A moist coating suggests that the *heat* in the body has not been severe enough to exhaust the body fluids. On the contrary, a dry yellow coating suggests that the body fluids have already been consumed by excessive *heat*.

The coating of a tongue may also appear grey or black, although these cases are very rare. A black tongue coating appears in the case of infectious diseases and indicates that the excess *heat* has penetrated deep into the body and has been transformed into *fire*, which exhausts the *yin*.

Listening and Smelling

This process comprises listening to the patient's voice, breathing and coughing, as well as smelling the odour of the patient's secretions and excretions. In Western medicine, these methods of diagnosis are sometimes used, but to a much smaller degree than in TCM.

Listening:

A low or feeble voice is often related to problems due to endogenous pathogenic factors indicating that a person is suffering from a *deficiency* syndrome. On the other hand, a loud voice is associated with exogenous insults to the body and *excess* syndromes. Restless and heavy breathing occurs in an *excess* syndrome, while feeble and short breaths are expected in a *deficiency* syndrome. Depressed patients have stagnant *qi* in the liver and often sigh. The detection of phlegm in one's cough is also important. An unproductive cough or a cough with little phlegm should be treated by eliminating the exogenous pathogenic factors from the lung.

Smelling:

This method of diagnosis also requires many years of experience. In general, any unusual or abnormal odours indicate an illness, but actual practice of this method is quite complex. Some examples of abnormal odours follow. Indigestion involving stale food in the stomach yields a strong unpleasant odour from the mouth. Foul-smelling sputum indicates that the doctor should suspect a lung abscess. Smelling the stool and urine is also valuable in disease diagnosis. A sour-smelling stool suggests the presence of *heat* in the intestine, while a fetid stool suggests *cold* in the intestine. Turbid and fetid urine is the manifestation of *damp heat* in the urinary bladder.

Inquiring

Inquiring is a diagnostic routine by which the clinical history and symptoms are collected in interviewing a patient. Information on the lifestyle, personality and living environment of the patient should be used as supplements to a patient's clinical history for diagnosis. The key points of a disease should be secured before elaborating on the details in the process of interrogation. This method is also used by Western doctors, however the way in which the information is utilized is quite different. There are several types of information which must be extracted during inquiry.

1. *The onset and progress of the illness*:
   Preliminary impressions of the illness as regards whether it is acute or chronic, active or latent, may be assessed from the patient's chief complaints.

2. *Exterior or interior to the body*:
   Exterior and *interior* are the two of the eight principal syndromes addressing the relative location and severity of the illnesses. The chief manifestations of an *exterior* syndrome are headache, aversion to cold and fever, while those of the *interior* syndrome are abdominal pain, diarrhea, vomiting, cold extremities, coma and mania. The above-mentioned symptoms must then be analyzed to find out whether the present illness is a new disease or a relapse, and whether the clinical condition is progressing uphill or downhill.

3. *Cold and heat*:
   Quite logically, chills are a symptom of diseases of the *cold* type while feverishness is common in diseases of the *heat* type. The location of the hotness or coldness is relevant. Chills in the skin, headache, muscle pain and fever are typical of *exterior cold*. Feeling cold inside the body or at the back and diarrhea are commonly

reported in diseases of the *interior cold* category. Inquiring about the location of the *heat* is done in a similar manner.

4. *Sweating*:
The output of sweat and the timing of sweating are important in disease differentiation. Patients with *exterior* syndromes are categorized as of an *exterior deficiency* type if there is sweating and as of an *exterior excess* type when sweating is absent. Diaphoretics should be used in the latter in order to stimulate perspiration but should not be prescribed for the former type of diseases. When sweating occurs determines whether the deficiency is related to the *yin* or the *yang*. Sweating after sleeping is a *yin deficiency*, and will stop in the daytime. Sweating during exertion is a *yang deficiency*. The treatment for these two types of diseases are different.

5. *Thirst*:
Those who are abnormally thirsty and drink a lot of water or those who especially like cold drinks have *interior heat* while those who do not drink much have *damp heat*. Patients who prefer hot drinks have *cold* in the middle *jiao*. Finally, those who are thirsty but have no desire to drink suffer from a deficiency of *kidney yin*.

6. *Diet*:
A patient's appetite can tell a doctor about the condition of the stomach and intestine. TCM pays much attention to the relation between appetite and diseases, recognizing that the acquired *qi* and nourishments are supplied by the spleen and stomach. Having a fair appetite suggests the *stomach qi* has not been depleted. Anorexia, constipation and fetid breath

occur when there is indigestion and food stasis in the stomach. Disease symptoms are more often aggravated and alleviated after food intake in *excess* and in *deficiency* syndromes respectively. Patients with a *cold* syndrome prefer hot food and vice versa for those suffering from a *heat* syndrome.

7. *Urination and defecation*:
   Inquiring about the patient's bowel and urinary activities serves to differentiate between *hot* and *cold* as well as *deficiency* and *excess* in TCM diagnosis. The colour and form of the faeces as well as the feeling upon defecation contribute useful information to clinical interpretation of illnesses. A hard and dry stool, a yellow or dark, extremely putrid and foul-smelling stool is typical of *excess* or *heat* syndromes. A loose stool mixed with undigested food, and a green or clay-coloured stool without pain on defecation suggest a *deficiency* or *cold* syndrome.

8. *Sleeping*:
   Somnolence and insomnia are mostly due to a de-ficiency and excess of *yang* respectively. Sleeplessness throughout the whole night represents a hyperactivity of *fire* in the liver and gallbladder or a disharmony between the heart and kidney. Fitful sleep is a mani-festation of deficiency of the heart and spleen. Sleep disorders may also be caused by disharmony between the small intestine and the stomach. However, infor-mation on sleep must be interpreted together with other clinical findings.

9. *Painful feeling in the chest and abdomen*:
   Pain, commonly located in the chest and abdomen, should be described in detail. Abrupt pain in the onset of a disease represents an *excess* syndrome. Chronic

pain is often reported in a *deficiency* syndrome and is usually mild. Severe pain or pain remaining at one site are more often reported in an *excess* syndrome. Pain found in a *deficiency* syndrome is attenuated by pressure but is aggravated in an *excess* syndrome.

10. *Menstruation*:
Certain illnesses inevitably affect normal menstruation, vaginal discharge and pregnancy. An unusually short menstrual cycle and the presence of large blood clots are related to a *heat* syndrome, whereas an abnormally long cycle is related to a *cold* syndrome. For women with dysmenorrhea or premenstrual pain denotes an *excess* syndrome, and pain after the period denotes a *deficiency* syndrome.

11. *Past history*:
It is important to refer to whether the patient's constitution is *hot* or *cold* before writing a prescription. In tracing the patient's past health, any history of major illnesses, chronic diseases and problems of the *zang-fu* organs should be recorded. In the pediatric age group, a history of measles and vaccinations should be available. The diet, lifestyle, habitat and hobbies as well as the patient's working environment should also be asked.

Palpation

Palpation is a form of diagnosis by feeling, touching and tapping on certain parts of the anatomy. Different emphasis is used according to the anatomy examined. This kind of diagnostic method is generally of relatively less importance in Western medicine. The dynamics of the pulse in TCM is very important in pulse diagnosis. Pain, tenderness and the presence of swelling are noted in palpating the abdomen. While feeling the skin, sweating, pain, redness and temperature of the limbs are to be watched. In TCM, as in Western medicine, pulse diagnosis is by far the most important form of palpation.

1. *Pulse diagnosis*:
    In performing pulse palpation, the doctor puts the index, middle and ring fingers on the radial artery. Three different grades of force, the light touch, the medium touch and the heavy touch are applied to the brachial pulse regions. In infants, the pulse is different from that of adults. The pulse may also be altered by exercise, alcohol and bathing. Half an hour's rest is recommended before palpation of the pulse.

    Several commonly encountered pulse types have been discovered through generations of TCM practice, and research has added complexity to pulse description. Out of a total of 28 classifications, there are about ten common and important types of pulse, each of which tells the doctor something about the nature of the disease. For example, a superficial pulse easily felt on the surface may indicate an *exterior* syndrome. A deep pulse only felt with a heavy touch is often found in *interior* syndromes. A slow pulse, slower than the normal rate of four to five beats per breath, is usually related to a *cold* syndrome. A rapid pulse is one which is six to seven beats per breath, and usually suggests the presence of a *heat* syndrome.

    As these descriptions show, the characteristics of the superficial and deep pulses define whether the disease affects the *exterior* or *interior* of the body. The slow pulse and rapid pulse differentiate whether the disease belongs to the *heat* or *cold* category. According to how much strength must be applied to feel the pulse, we can tell whether the disease is one of *excess* or *deficiency*.

In addition, a very feeble pulse, a full pulse, a soft pulse, a hesitant pulse, along with many other types are possible, but will not be elaborated on here. Additional information on the excess or deficiency of *qi* and *blood* can be ascertained from feeling the pulse.

2. *Palpation of the body surface*:
Sweat is detected by touching the skin surface. Palpation also serves to detect the presence of pus and its location. Pus is present if a swelling is both hot and yielding and is absent when the swelling is cold and solid. Tenderness upon a light touch suggests the pus is located superficially. Pain on deep palpation suggests the contrary and indicates that the pus probably lies deep underneath.

3. *Palpation of the four limbs*:
Feeling the temperature of the limbs can tell the status of *yang qi* in the body. If the lower part of the hand is warm, this suggests that the illness is caused by exogenous pathogens. Warmth in the palms ascribes a disease to internal pathogens. Infants should be observed for signs of convulsion if their fingertips feel cold despite a high body temperature. Measles should be suspected if there are additional signs of cough and conjunctivitis.

4. *Palpation of the chest and abdomen*:
Palpation is done at a point located beneath the left breast. A normal pulsation should be easily felt and is forceful on palpation, indicating that the *pectoral qi* is stored in the chest. A feeble pulse difficult to palpate suggests that the *pectoral qi* is weak. A fast beat denotes a leaking of the *pectoral qi*. Abdominal distension with tenderness is evidence of an *excess* syndrome. A soft abdomen or abdominal pain atten-

uated by pressure denotes a *deficiency* syndrome.

In summary, the four diagnostic methods (inspection, listening and smelling, inquiring and palpation) have their own unique functions in the clinical approach to disease. Information collected from the four methods should be analyzed as a whole and interpreted with cross-referencing to one another. It would be ideal if the four methods concur with each other in diagnosis. However, when the pulse diagnosis disagrees with that of the other methods, then one has to decide which to follow. There is no hard and fast rule to follow in the use of the four diagnostic types. Only through experience and thorough understanding of the fundamental principles of TCM can one guarantee mastery of the four methods in clinical analysis.

Differentiation of Syndromes according to the Eight Principles

The Eight Principles refer to *yin* and *yang*, *exterior* and *interior*, *cold* and *heat*, *deficiency* and *excess*. They are fundamental theories in TCM and are extensively applied in its practice. These principles are the guidelines for the analysis of a disease so that appropriate treatment is given to a patient. For a common symptom like a headache, the illness may be attributed to *cold*, *heat*, *deficiency* or *excess*. Treating *cold* syndromes inappropriately with *cold*-natured drugs instead of *heat*-natured drugs will only aggravate the symptoms. Treatment according to the Eight Principles aids in deciding on the appropriate choice of drugs. This type of TCM practice is therefore very different from the simple practice of symptomatic relief which does not offer definitive cure of the illness.

Yin and Yang

Yin and yang describe the opposite properties of all things. The presentation, the clinical course of a disease and the psychic status of a patient may be interpreted according to the understanding of yin and yang. In fact yin and yang also encompass the eight principles. Exterior, heat and excess are ascribed to yang, while interior, cold and deficiency are ascribed to yin. As yin and yang may describe the dual properties of the universe, the mechanism and presentation of an illness is discussed in terms of this dual concept, which offers a simple and practical guide for the treatment of diseases.

In the yin-yang theory, typical yin-yang pairs are interior/exterior, downward/upward, ventrum/dorsum, bone-and-flesh/skin, the five zang/six fu organs and blood/qi. In yang syndromes, the symptoms are strong and vigorous and the qi is hyperactive, whereas the contrary is observed in the yin syndromes (Chapter 2). Thus patients acquiring yang syndromes are feverish, hyperactive and their pulses are superficial, rolling, full and active while those with yin syndromes are chilly, quiet and the pulses are deep, weak, thready and hesitant. It is inappropriate to have yang signs in a yin syndrome or vice versa. In fact, the prognosis occasionally may be told by analyzing the yin-yang of the disease. A famous Chinese physician once said, "Those with a yin syndrome and a yang pulse survive, while those with a yang syndrome and a yin pulse die". The presence of a yin pulse in patients with a yang syndrome suggests that an exogenous pathogenic factor in the interior of the body has emerged to the exterior. A good prognosis is expected even if the disease looks serious. On the other hand, a yang pulse in a yin syndrome implies that the exogenous pathogenic factor has invaded into the *interior* of the body and the prognosis is guarded, no matter how mild the illness is. Thus it is important to ascertain the amount of *yang qi* in monitoring the course of an illness.

Exterior and Interior

The *exterior* and *interior* refer to the location of the body affected by the disease. This pair may also refer to the severity of the illness. The *exterior* comprises the skin and meridians, and is the location first invaded by exogenous factors. The typical complaints of an *exterior* syndrome are aversion to cold, fever, headache, a stuffy nose and myalgia. As the pathogenic factor penetrates the *interior* or the *zang-fu* organs, symptoms of an *interior* syndrome emerge. The manifestations of this are high fever, restlessness, delirium, vomiting, diarrhea, abdominal pain, urine retention and constipation. Differentiation between *exterior* and *interior* syndrome is therefore very important. The former implies that the pathogenic factors are staying away from the *interior zang-fu* organs and not yet affecting the *blood* or *qi*. In other words, the illness is relatively mild and the correct treatment by diaphoresis may easily drive away the pathogenic factors from the body and cure the disease. Once the pathogenic factors have invaded deep into the *interior*, applying the same treatment not only fails to drive away the pathogens lying deep in the *interior*, but also acquires the negative effect of harming the *yang qi* in the *exterior*. For *interior* syndromes, mediation or purgation treatment methods should be used instead.

Exterior and *interior* can also be subdivided into *cold* and *heat*, *deficiency* and *excess* as shown in the following table:

Exterior		
Cold	Aversion to cold	*Deficiency* (Sweating) *Excess* (No sweating)
Heat	Absence of aversion to cold	*Deficiency* (Sweating) *Excess* (No sweating)

Interior		
Cold	Not thirsty, desire to put on more clothes	*Deficiency* (Weak and slow pulse) *Excess* (Forceful and slow pulse)
Heat	Thirsty, desire to drink and put on less clothes	*Deficiency* (Weak and rapid pulse) *Excess* (Forceful and rapid pulse)

Symptoms of the patient may be differentiated into *exterior* or *interior* according to the table above. It should be noted that symptoms of *exterior* and *interior* may occur at the same time in a patient. Illness involving both the *exterior* and *interior* manifests a combination of both syndromes. In TCM terminology, we ascribe this phenomenon to both the *exterior* and *interior* being sick. Clinical management should only be decided on after referring to other symptoms and signs. A more elaborate differentiation between *exterior* or *interior* is necessary for determining which to treat first and how to treat them according to the Eight Principles. There is yet another syndrome not entirely compatible with both *exterior* and *interior* syndromes. This is the *intermediate* syndrome showing intermittent fever and chills, discomfort and fullness in the chest and hypochondrium, irritability and nausea, bitter taste in the mouth, anorexia, dry throat, dizziness and string-taut pulse. Neither diaphoresis nor purgation, but only mediation should be used in the treatment.

Cold and Heat

In TCM, *cold* and *heat* are not defined by the body temperature. There is *cold* in the *exterior* of a patient suffering from chills, how high the body temperature is. *Warm*-natured drugs which induce sweating may therefore be used. Diseases of a *cold* nature require *warm*-natured drugs, while diseases of a *heat*-nature require *cold*-natured drugs. This principle should be followed carefully in the prescription of drugs. Misidentification of the nature of the disease and thereby using drugs of the wrong nature will only make the patient worse.

The distinctions between a *cold* syndrome and a *heat* syndrome are shown on the following page:

Careful analysis is required in order to differentiate between *heat* and *cold* accurately according to their complex presentations. It is normal for a dehydrated person to pass concentrated yellow urine. Such a phenomenon should not be counted as a manifestation of a *heat* syndrome. However, if the urine output remains low and the colour is still dark after rehydration, then there would be no doubt of the diagnosis of a *heat* syndrome. Similarly, passing clear urine persistently after the limitation of water intake is diagnostic of a *cold* syndrome. These are examples of how to tell the *cold* or *heat* nature of a disease. The following is an introduction of defining *cold* and *heat* with reference to the constitution of an individual's physique.

A Cold Constitution:

A *cold* constitution and a *yang* deficiency often come

	Cold syndrome	*Heat* syndrome
Tolerance & intolerance	Cold intolerance, wearing excess clothes, does not drink much water	Heat intolerance, wearing less clothes than usual, drinks a lot of water
Urination & defecation [1]	Loose stool with undigested food, clear and profuse urine	Dry stool, abdominal pain, diarrhea
Four limbs [2]	Cold extremities	Warm extremities
Tongue coating [3]	White and moist coating	Yellow and dry coating
Pulse	Mostly a slow pulse	Mostly a rapid pulse

Notes:

[1] In patients with a *heat* syndrome, there is functional hyperactivity in the *zang-fu* organs with an increased consumption of body fluid. The patient may complain of constipation, oliguria and occasionally hematuria. On the contrary, loose stool or stool with undigested food, clear and profuse urine occur in the patients with a *cold* syndrome because of functional hypoactivity and a low water consumption.

[2] The four limbs, where *yang qi* gathers, are apt to reflect the state of *cold* and *heat*. Patients with *heat* have warm limbs, while patients with *cold* have cold limbs even in warm weather.

[3] Yellow, greasy and dry coating may also appear in a *dampness* syndrome. Thus the *cold* and *heat* should be determined by the overall clinical picture rather than the tongue coating as it is.

together. There is an old teaching which says that *"external cold* is caused by a *yang* deficiency". As mentioned in Chapter 2, *yang* denotes heat and power; the deficiency of which defers the assimilation of energy and heat production. A person with such a constitution is more prone to catching colds. Various signs of a functional deficiency may then appear, such as pallor, cold extremities, aversion to cold, lassitude, shortness of breath, a loose stool, and clear and profuse urine.

A Heat Constitution:

A *heat* constitution is directly related to a *yin* deficiency. In TCM, there is an understanding that "a *yin* deficiency ignites internal *heat*". *Yin* denotes body fluids, the deficiency of which depletes the *yin fluids*. Lack of moistening by the body fluids can cause headaches, toothaches, aphthous ulcers, constipation, hemorrhoids, yellow urine and an aversion to *heat*.

Patients with a *heat* constitution are more prone to contracting *heat* symptoms. *Cold* symptoms occur more frequently in patients with a *cold* constitution. Taking these into consideration, *hot* and *cold* herbs should be used with caution on patients with *heat* and *cold* constitutions respectively.

Deficiency and Excess

Deficiency and *excess* essentially describes the state of the *genuine qi* in the body. A person is said to have *deficiency* when the *genuine qi* is depleted for whatever reason. Since in TCM the proper balance of *qi* and *blood* is believed to keep diseases at bay, it is easy to see why an *excess* or *deficiency* of *qi* can be a factor in causing illness. According to a classical TCM teaching, *"Excess* exists when exogenous pathogens dominate". This is conceivable because *genuine qi* is generated in excess as a reaction to or as a defence mechanism against pathogenic insults. In TCM treatment, a *deficiency* requires replenishing the *qi* while inhibiting measures should be taken when there is *an excess*. Differentiation between *deficiency* and *excess* is therefore necessary before choosing either the replenishment or inhibition form of treatment. In the clinical approach to a disease, emphasis is put more on *deficiency-excess* than *cold-heat*.

Bearing in mind why we have to differentiate between *deficiency* and *excess*, the following is a guideline on how this may be achieved:

1.   A new or acute disease is usually due to an excess of pathogens, which then requires inhibiting drugs. Deficiency of *genuine qi* is common after a chronic illness. The appropriate treatment is to reinforce the *qi* with appropriate drugs.

2.   The body build: A slim and weak build is associated with a deficiency of *qi* whereas a person with a strong build rarely suffers from *deficiency*; an *excess* is much more likely to be encountered.

3.   The pulse: The pulse offers useful information concerning *excess-deficiency*. In long-standing illnesses, the pulse is usually weak (*deficiency*) and strong in acute or newly acquired illnesses (*excess*).

4.   Miscellaneous: Other symptoms should be considered at the same time in the process of differentiation. Abdominal pain is an example. Abdominal pain occurring before but subsiding after diarrhea is accounted for by a stagnancy in the gut. The stagnancy is the pathogen which suggests that there is an *excess*. However, when the pain persists after diarrhea or when

there is continuous diarrhea or malabsorption, then there is a *deficiency* of *qi*. Similarly, premenstrual pain is an *excess* whereas dysmenorrhea persisting after menstruation is a *deficiency*.

In actual practice, simple *deficiency* or *excess* is uncommon. A combination of both is much more likely to be encountered. It is important to decide which one of the combinations is of primary importance so that priority can be given to either inhibiting the *excess* or reinforcing the *deficiency*. In the former, pathogens are dominating and hence the method of elimination should be taken as the primary goal in treatment. In the latter, when anti-pathogenic *genuine qi* is deprived, the method of *qi* reinforcement should be used. The proper choice of treatment certainly accelerates the recovery of the patient. It would be undesirable to misuse the purgation method in patients with *deficiency* or employ wrongly the nourishing method in patients with *excess*. Accurate differentiation between *deficiency* and *excess* should always be emphasized in clinical practice.

Differentiation of Syndromes according to the Theory of the Six Meridians

This diagnostic approach attempts to locate where the pathology lies in the meridian system of the body.(See Chapter 9 for a complete explanation of meridians.) The six meridians comprise the three *yangs* (*Taiyang, Yangming* and *Shaoyang*) and the three *yins* (*Taiyin, Shaoyin* and

Jueyin). The meridian system is an elaboration of the *yin-yang* system, hence differentiation between *yin* and *yang* comes before assigning the disease to any of the six meridian syndromes.

As mentioned in the beginning of this chapter, illnesses with an excess of *qi*, acute or febrile illnesses are ascribed to *yang* while those with a deficiency of *qi*, chronic illnesses or *cold* manifestations are ascribed to *yin*. Thus the symptoms of the three *yang* meridian syndromes correspond with those of the *excess* or *heat* syndromes while the three *yin* meridian syndromes concur mostly with the *deficiency* or *cold* syndromes. Each of the six meridians has its own symptoms when diseased, therefore knowing how to differentiate between them is very valuable in diagnosis.

The Taiyang Syndrome

The *Taiyang* syndrome is an *exterior* syndrome related to acute febrile illnesses. The common symptoms are aversion to cold, headache, myalgia, fever and stiff pain in the back and neck. The pulse is usually superficial. Those who sweat a lot, are averse to wind chill and bear superficial and slow pulses are suffering from the *Taiyang-wind* syndrome. Those who do not sweat and their pulses are superficial and tense are suffering from the *Taiyang-cold* syndrome.

The Yangming Syndrome

The *Yangming* syndrome occurs at the peak of febrile illnesses when the pathogens have already invaded the *interior*. Typical symptoms are fever, sweating without chills, aversion to heat, thirst and constipation. The pulse is often full and forceful. Hyperpyrexia, profuse sweating, extreme thirst and forceful pulse are signs that the *heat* pathogenic factors have extensively involved the meridian system of the body, yielding typical manifestations of the *Yangming* meridian syndrome. When there are afternoon fever, sweating of the limbs, abdominal distension and pain, constipation, rough yellow or black tongue coating, and deep, slow and *excess*-type pulses, the *heat* has already joined with the wastes in the intestine to harm the *fu* organs. All this constitutes the *Yangming fu* syndrome.

The Shaoyang Syndrome

The *Shaoyang* syndrome is an intermediate form in which the pathogenic factors and the *genuine qi* have their confrontation between the *exterior* and *interior* compartments of the body. The manifestations are thus somewhat in between those belonging to the *exterior* and *interior* syndromes. Typical symptoms and signs are fever alternating with chills, bitter taste in the mouth, dry mouth, fullness in the chest and costal pain, blurring of vision, vomiting and a string-taut pulse.

The Taiyin Syndrome

The *Taiyin* syndrome is an amalgam of *deficiency* and *cold* in the *interior* body compartment. This is the mildest syndrome among the three *yin* syndromes and is usually due to a deficiency of the spleen after an insult by pathogenic factors. The corresponding symptoms are distending pain in the abdomen, vomiting, diarrhea, anorexia and a weak pulse.

The Shaoyin Syndrome

The *Shaoyin* syndrome is a more serious form in which *deficiency* and *cold* have already spread to the whole body. The presentation is therefore more serious than that found in the *Taiyin* syndrome. The patient has insomnia, chills, cold extremities and a weak thready pulse.

The Jueyin Syndrome

The exhaustion of *genuine qi* allows subtle changes in signs and symptoms. It is common to find in the *Jueyin* syndrome swinging body temperature, chills and rigour, anorexia, irritability, dyspnea or choking feeling in the chest, vomiting and diarrhea.

Differentiation of Syndromes according to the Theory of *Wei, Qi, Ying* and *Xue*

This is a grading of the stages of febrile illnesses from the least to the most serious in the sequence of *wei, qi, ying* and *xue*.

Syndrome of the Wei Stage

This is characterized by fever, mild chills, headache, coughs, thirst, thin white tongue coating and superficial pulses. The description is comparable to that of the *exterior* syndrome.

Syndrome of the Qi Stage

The *exterior* symptoms have already evolved into *interior* manifestations of fever with aversion to heat, sweating, thirst, coughs, shortness of breath, yellow tongue coating and rolling rapid or full pulses.

Syndrome of the Ying Stage

The patient appears to be stuporous, disorientated or

unconscious. The skin temperature is high, the conjunctiva is injected, the breath is heavy, the lips are dry, the tongue is intensely red and without coating, and the pulse rate is fast.

Syndrome of the Xue Stage

There are skin rashes, epistaxis, hematemesis, blood in stool and hematuria or seizure. The tongue is red and dry while the pulse is fast and thready.

Both the meridian diagnosis and the *wei, qi, ying, xue* diagnosis essentially apply to the management of infectious diseases. In combination with the Eight Principles, the character and the location of the disease may then be assessed.

Differentiation of Syndromes according to the Theory of the *Zang-fu* Organs

All diseases may be ascribed to either exogenous pathogenic factors or internal injury. Diseases due to exogenous pathogenic factors are usually differentiated according to the theory of the six meridians and the theory of *wei, qi, ying, xue*, while the diseases caused by internal injury are differentiated according to the theory of the *zang-fu* organs. Owing to the mutual dependency and inter-relations of the individual *zang-fu* organs, complications involving more than one organ are commonly encountered. The *zang-fu* theory provides a diagnostic means by which the site of the disease may be located and by which the nature of involvement of an individual organ may be assessed.

Syndromes of the *zang-fu* organs are described as follows.

Heart and Small Intestine

Symptom complexes of the heart can further be differentiated in greater detail for writing prescription.

1. *Deficiency of heart yin* or *heart blood*: Pallor, poor memory, insomnia, dream-disturbed sleep, early waking, palpitation, pink tongue with little coating, thready and weak pulse are the typical manifestations. In the presence of *internal heat*, there will be flushing of the face and limbs, hot feelings in the extremities and the chest, night sweats, a red and uncoated tongue, thready and rapid pulses.

2. *Deficiency of heart-yang or heart-qi*: Typical symptoms and signs are palpitation, shortness of breath, weakness and lassitude, aversion to cold, spontaneous sweating, somnolence but light sleep, and a pale tongue. The pulses are thready, weak and of the *deficiency* type.

3. *Hyperactivity of the heart fire or heart-heat*: The patient complains of palpitation, insomnia, dysphoria and thirst. There may be aphthous ulcer at the tip of the tongue and lips. The urine colour is deep yellow, the tongue is red, and the pulses are rapid.

4. *Phlegm misting the heart*: The patient may be unconscious or comatose, or may have unreasoned weeping or laughing. There may be gurgling sound with sputum in the throat. The tongue has a greasy yellow coating and the pulses are rapid.

Table 3   The Physiology and Pathology of the Heart and
Small Intestine

	Physiological functions	Pathological Manifestations
Heart	1. Houses the mind	Mental confusion, amnesia, insomnia, palpitation, loss of consciousness, delirium, depression, mania, unreasonable weeping and laughing
	2. Dominates the blood and vessels	Extravasation of blood, hemorrhagic diseases, anemia
	3. Is reflected in the tongue	Tip of the tongue will be red in the case of *heart-heat*, and pale in the case of deficiency of the *heart-blood*
	4. Sweat is the fluid of the heart	Profuse sweating leading to collapse of the *heart yang*, and deficiency of *heart yin* resulting in hyperactivity of *heart yang* and night sweats
	5. Has an *interior-exterior* relation with the small intestine	*Heat* shifts to the small intestine, causing scanty urine and hematuria
Small Intestine	1. Distinguishes between the clear and the turbid	Diarrhea and abdominal pain
	2. Responsible for urine excretion	Hematuria, dysuria and pain in the penis

Liver and Gallbladder

Table 4   The Physiology and Pathology of the Liver and Gallbladder

	Physiological functions	Pathological manifestations
Liver	1. Acts as a vital organ	Behavioral disorder, vertigo and dizziness
	2. Stores blood	Extravasation of blood
	3. Controls the tendons	Opistotonus, convulsion, spasticity, peripheral cyanosis
	4. Is reflected in the eyes	Swollen eyes, blurring of vision and dry eyes in the case of a *liver blood deficiency*
	5. Relates to the *Jueyin* meridian, which passes around the genitalia and the breasts	Hypochondriac and testicular pain, hernia and breast symptoms
	6. Relates to *wind*	Dizziness, seizures, coma
	7. Has an *interior-exterior* relation with the gallbladder	Presence of *liver fire* shows gallbladder symptoms such as headache, deafness, vomiting
Gall-bladder	1. Acts as a mediator organ	Indecisiveness and timidness
	2. *Gallbladder fire* interacts with *liver fire*	Headache, blurred vision, bitter taste in the mouth

Common syndromes ascribed to the liver in detail are:

1.   **Liver qi:** Stagnation of *liver qi* due to seven emotional factors may cause referral pain in the costal regions, epigastric fullness and distending discomfort radiating to the lower abdomen and string-taut pulses.

2. *Liver yang*: Dizziness, blurring of vision, tinnitus and bitter taste in the mouth may appear in the case of hyperactivity of *liver yang*.

3. *Liver fire*: Severe headache, red, swollen and painful eyes, dark or red urine, yellow tongue coating are typical symptoms. The pulses are string-taut, rapid or forceful.

4. *Liver wind*: The patient may have dizziness, blurring of vision, twitching of eyelids, spasm of tendons and muscles, numbness, convulsion, opisthotonus, string-taut rapid pulses. Apoplexy may occur if the *liver wind* is vigorous.

Spleen and Stomach

Common syndromes ascribed to the spleen and stomach are:

1. *Yang deficiency of the spleen and stomach*: Diarrhea after meals, loss of appetite.

2. *Yin deficiency of the spleen and stomach*: A red tongue, dry stool, tastelessness in the mouth, loss of appetite.

3. *Hyperactivity of the stomach yang and hypoactivity of the spleen yang*: The former is a result of the latter. The former gives rise to insatiable hunger while the latter renders stool loose and causes diarrhea.

4. *Invasion of the spleen by dampness*: Fullness and distention in the epigastric region, heaviness of the four limbs and the body, thick greasy tongue coating.

5. *Deficiency of the spleen leading to phlegm*: Coughing with profuse sputum, rolling pulse and greasy tongue coating.

Table 5   The Physiology and Pathology of the Spleen and Stomach

	Physiological Functions	Pathological Manifestations
Spleen	1. Controls the digestion and assimilation of nutrients	Indigestion, fullness and distension in the abdomen, loose stool and edema
	2. Controls the blood	Bleeding disorders such as menorrhagia
	3. Dominates the muscles and the four limbs	Emaciation, lassitude
	4. Controls the ascent of the *spleen qi*	Descent of *qi* results in diarrhea, loss of interest in and taste of food
Stomach	1. Accommodates food and digestion	Dyspepsia, anorexia and weight loss in the case of hyperactivity of *stomach fire*
	2. Controls the descent of the *stomach qi*	Ascent of *qi* results in nausea, vomiting and belching

Lung and Large Intestine

Common syndromes ascribed to the lung are:

1. *Deficiency of lung yin*: Dry throat, hoarse voice, unproductive cough, red tongue and thready rapid pulses.

2. *Deficiency of lung qi*: Pallor, feeble voice, short breath, spontaneous sweating, aversion to cold, susceptibility to cold, cough and asthma, pale tongue and soft pulse.

3. *Invasion of the lung by wind cold*: Aversion to cold and wind, clear nasal discharge, cough with mucoid sputum, superficial pulses and a thin white tongue coating.

4. *Lung heat*: Flushed face, paroxysmal cough, perinasal boil, thick purulent sputum, a yellow tongue coating and rapid pulses.

Table 6   The Physiology and Pathology of the Lung and Large Intestine

	Physiological Functions	Pathological manifestations
Lung	1. Dominates the *qi*	Deficiency of *lung qi* causes shortness of breath
	2. Controls the descent of the *lung qi*	Ascent of *qi* results in coughing, wheezing, asthma
	3. Guards the skin and hair	Prone to invasion by exogenous pathogenic factor
	4. Is reflected in the nose and related to voice	Stuffy nose, nasal discharge, sneezing, hoarseness of voice
	5. Regulates water flow and keeps the fluids descending to the bladder	Oliguria, edema
	6. Has an *exterior-interior* relation with the large intestine	Constipation, blood in the stool
Large Intestine	Defecation	Dry hard stool, diarrhea

Kidney and Urinary Bladder

Table 7   The Physiology and Pathology of the Kidney
and Bladder

	Physiological Functions	Pathological Manifestations
Kidney	1. Strengthens physiological functions	Inefficiency at work, slow movements, poor memory, dementia
	2. Stores the *essence* of the *zang-fu* organs and the gonads	Hypofunction of the *zang-fu* organs in chronic illnesses, seminal emission and spermatorrhoea
	3. Moderates the bones and teeth	Osteoporosis, kyphosis, loosening of teeth
	4. Is reflected in the ear and the hair	Tinnitus, deafness, brittle hair, alopecia
	5 Is related to the back	Back pain
	6. Controls the perineum	Dysuria, urinary incontinence, morning diarrhea
Bladder	Regulates *fluids*	Difficult urination, turbid urine or urethral discharge

The common manifestations of the kidney syndrome are low back pain, tinnitus, deafness, brittle hair or alopecia, loose teeth, weak legs, impotence, seminal emission, morning diarrhea , aversion to cold and poor memory.

Common syndromes ascribed to the kidney are:

1. *Decline of the Mingmen fire*: The *kidney yang*, being the source of life, is called the *Mingmen fire*. Deficiency of the *fire* may have manifestations of cold aversion and cold extremities, lassitude, somnolence, weak legs, back pain, edema, impotence, spermatorrhoea, a pale flabby tongue and deep thready weak pulses.

2. *Hyperactivity of the ministerial fire*: A special type of *ministerial fire* is supposed to have its origin in the kidney and is sent off to the *zang-fu* organs to nourish the whole body. Deficiency of *yin* of the liver and kidney may be complicated with the hyperactivity of the *ministerial fire*. The patient may complain of wakeful sleeps interfered by dreams, penile erection and nocturnal ejaculation.

3. *Deficiency of kidney yin*: Burning sensation in the chest, palms and soles, afternoon fever, dryness and pain in the throat, hoarse voice, night sweats, nocturnal ejaculation, a patchy tongue coating, tongue fissuring and thready rapid pulses.

Conclusion

Clinical management in TCM essentially depends on the analysis of disease by means of the *zang-fu* theories and the Eight Principles. In contrast to Western medicine, TCM theories do not refer to genuine anatomy or specific organs. The *zang-fu* organs represent functional units rather than anatomical structures. Much effort has been put into comparing both schools of medical practice. For example, it has recently been discovered that kidney deficiency is analogous to endocrine disorders, with particular reference to adrenal, thyroid and gonadal insufficiencies. The association of ageing with decreased sex hormone production is compatible with TCM sayings like "the kidney stores the essence" and "the kidney governs reproduction". Despite such findings of concurrence between TCM and Western medicine, the differences in how a doctor goes about diagnosing a patient are still great indeed.

7

PRINCIPLES OF TREATMENT AND PRESCRIPTION

Strategy for the Definitive Treatment of Disease

TCM aims beyond the symptomatic treatment of diseases. Treatment is decided on after analyzing symptoms or symptom complexes according to the basic TCM principles. In the case of fever, for instance, antipyretic treatment comprises more than simple use of *cold*-natured medicine or antipyretics. Fever is regarded as a manifestation of any number of illnesses caused by a variety of pathogens such as *wind cold, warmness, summer-heat, phlegm, yin deficiency, stagnation of qi,* and internal impairment caused by overstrain and parasitic infestation. The choice of drugs thus varies accordingly. A febrile patient with a *yin* deficiency treated with *cold*-natured drugs not only will not be cured of the fever, but may in fact experience side-effects from the drugs. Only after careful differentiation of the symptoms can an accurate diagnosis be reached and the underlying cause be found to achieve the best treatment possible for the patient.

Search for the fundamental cause of an illness is emphasized in order to accomplish definitive treatment. TCM thus introduces the essential concept of "fundamentals and ramifications". For a patient, the body is the fundamental while the disease is a ramification. For the disease per se, its underlying cause is the fundamental, whereas its manifestations are the ramifications. In the practice of TCM, in treatment, priority is given to the patient and not to the symptoms. In other words, removing the fundamental cause of a disease is more important than symptomatic relief. From a clinical point of view, symptoms contracted first are fundamentals while those that follow are the ramifications. From the point of view of localization, diseases involving the *interior* or the *zang-fu* organs are the fundamentals, whereas diseases limited to the *exterior* are ramifications. In TCM, distinguishing fundamentals from the ramifications is useful in determining the priority of treatment.

An example is a patient with symptoms which point to a deficiency of the spleen and stomach, inadequacy of the bladder *qi* as well as the presence of *damp heat*. Tracking the natural sequence of the disease mechanism, the most fundamental would be a deficiency of the spleen and stomach, which gives rise to *damp heat* symptoms. The *damp heat* descends to the lower *jiao* affecting the bladder. Inadequacy of the bladder *qi* is a ramification of the spleen and stomach. The countercurrent flow of *qi* thereby affects the lung and results in dyspnea. Hence dyspnea in this case is the ultimate ramification of the other ramifications (bladder and *damp heat*). Similarly, deficiency of the spleen and stomach is the fundamental of the fundamentals (bladder and *damp heat*).

As stated earlier, treating the fundamental cause of a disease is most important. However, when the acute symptoms are serious, treatment may be designated to the ramification instead of the fundamental. A patient suffering from a chronic illness may be invaded by an exogenous pathogen. The acute symptoms, though being a ramification, should be treated first. At an early stage of ramification, the exogenous pathogen has not yet affected the *qi* and *blood*. It is not difficult to remove the exogenous pathogen at this stage. It would be undesirable to hold off the treatment until the exogenous pathogen has depleted the *qi*, the *blood* and finally the *genuine qi*. Early treatment of the ramification is therefore required when the symptoms effectively prevent the *genuine qi* from being depressed.

Dosage

Estimation of the dosage of drugs often depends on the status of the *genuine qi* rather than the severity of the disease. An acutely ill patient with severe symptom may still have intact *genuine qi*. A heavy dose is recommended for somebody whose *genuine qi* is full. On the contrary, a mildly sick patient may be weak in *genuine qi*. A light or sparing dose should be used in this case, since too great a dosage would be like overwatering a withering plant. The choice of drug dosage depends therefore on the intactness of *genuine qi*.

In summary, the primary aim from what we have discussed is to preserve the *genuine qi*.

The Physical Constitution of the Patient

It is inevitable that some people have a weaker body constitution than others. With respect to the varying drug properties and the physique of the patient, due consideration should be given to the dose and the *hot-cold* nature of the prescribed drugs. For residents in North China where the climate is cold, strong diaphoretics, or drugs for the treatment of an *exterior* syndrome, such as Herba Ephedrae and cinnamon twigs may be used and a relatively heavy dose may be recommended. In the warmer South China, for the same clinical conditions, mulberry leaf and Herba Schizonepeta are preferable; and a moderate dose is advisable. Age, as well as one's constitution, must also be considered. For example, the *attacking* method (see next section) should be avoided in the elderly whose *yin* and *yang* are deficient and who are vulnerable to exhaustion by drugs. A physically strong person, such as a relatively young manual worker, would have no ill effects from the *attacking* method of drug prescription.

The presentation of a disease varies according to individual patients and throughout the course of the disease. Even within a patient, symptoms may be quite inconsistent at different stages of a disease. Treatment should be decided upon according to the clinical status of a patient. It would be fallacious to apply indiscriminately a standard prescription to treat a disease in different patients no matter how effective it is said to be.

Guidelines of Treatment for
Deficiency and *Excess*

The method of *reinforcing* is usually used on a patient who is chronically ill and deficient in *genuine qi*. *Reinforcing* is the opposite of *attacking*, and means that the drugs prescribed will have the effect of strengthening the patient, whereas *attacking* means that the drugs are meant to destroy the cause or causes of illness. Those who are acutely ill and are dominated by pathogens but without a *genuine qi* deficiency should be treated with the *attacking* method. On the other hand, the *reinforcing* method is not indicated when pathogens are dominating. If a patient is in an abrupt *deficiency* status complicated by an acute illness, use of the *attacking* method should be deferred until the *deficiency* is remedied by reinforcement. Conversely, chronically ill patients whose *qi* is deficient and have *excess* symptoms should be managed by attacking gently the latter while reinforcing the former. Thus according to the TCM treatment principle, it is essential to consider the clinical features with respect to rapidity in onset and steadiness in progress, and to differentiate between the fundamental and ramified symptoms before writing a prescription for a patient.

Fundamental Methods of
Treatment

Oral administration is the most widely used route of administration of drugs in clinical practice. In this chapter, the eight fundamental methods of treatment are briefly described as follows.

The Diaphoretic Method

Diaphoresis is a treatment method for an *exterior* syndrome, using drugs to dissipate the exogenous pathogenic factors from the *exterior* through sweat induction. Exogenous pathogenic factors invade the body through the skin (*exterior*) and then penetrate further into the *interior*. Early treatment to expel the pathogen should begin before the *interior* is involved, otherwise the diaphoretic method would not work and should no longer be used. Diaphoresis may vary according to the patient's physique as well as clinical conditions and chronicity of the illness. In patients with a *yin* deficiency and *external* symptoms, simple diaphoresis may aggravate the *yin* deficiency due to body fluid loss. On the other hand, just nourishing the *yin* may retain the exogenous pathogen. The best compromise would be enhancing the *yin* at the time of diaphoresis by adding *yin*-promoting drugs.

The Emetic Method

Emesis or vomit induction may be used when noxious substances accumulate in the chest or abdomen and fail to be expelled by means of diaphoresis or purgation. It may also be applied to patients with excessive phlegm or those who have consumed poisons. However, emesis significantly damages the *primary qi* and should be avoided as far as possible in patients with a weak constitution.

The Purgative Method

Purgation gets rid of what is retained in the body and is good for the normal turnover of the body as well as dissipation of *heat* and pain in the body. The purgation method is useful whenever there is stagnancy in the stomach with or without abdominal distension, or when there is fluid in the abdominal or pleural cavity, blood stasis, intestinal obstruction and acute pancreatitis. The purgation method should only be used in *excess* syndromes and should be applied to patients with a strong constitution; otherwise undesirable results may occur. Strong purgative drugs should not be used on the elderly or those with constipation. Instead, a mild purgative is recommended so as to avoid inducing dehydration or worsening the constipation.

The Mediation Method

Mediation is a therapeutic method applicable to cases where the exogenous pathogenic factors neither exist in the *exterior* nor in the *interior*. Mediation therapy serves various purposes. It alleviates pathogens in semi-*exterior* and semi-*interior* syndromes to check their penetration in the *interior*. It also restores the balance between *yin* and *yang* and harmonizes the *blood* and *qi*. Mediation comprises therapeutic measures not available from the other seven treatment methods.

The Warming Method

Warming is a method by which *warm*-natured or *heat*-natured drugs are used to eliminate *cold* in the body and to fortify the *yang qi*. There are two different warming methods. One is to recover the depleted *yang* so as to rescue a patient from collapse. This should be introduced to patients with an impending collapse of *yang* as suggested by phenomena such as aversion to cold, huddling up, vomiting and diarrhea, profuse sweating, cold extremities as well as a deep and hidden pulse. Another approach is to warm the middle *jiao* so as to dispel *cold*. This method is applicable to patients with *yang* deficiency in the spleen and stomach who complain of a cold sensation in the epigastrium and cold extremities, who prefer hot drinks or who have a loose stool.

Once the *yang qi* in the middle *jiao* is stimulated by *warm*-natured drugs, the *cold* will vanish by itself. The warming method is exclusively for *cold* syndromes and is contraindicated whenever there are evidences of *heat* syndrome or a hyperactive *deficiency fire* in the *interior*, such as a red tongue, a dry and sore throat, hematemesis and the presence of blood in stool.

The Heat-clearing Method

This is a method of clearing the excessive *internal heat* with *cold*-natured medicines after the exogenous pathogenic factors are dispelled. However, the *heat*-clearing method should be used with caution in subjects with *heat* syndrome but with a weak spleen and stomach, poor appetite and a loose stool.

The Elimination Method

Elimination has the dual purpose of dispelling pathogens and dissipating stagnancy. The treatment is directed against accumulation and stagnancy of *qi*, blood, phlegm and food. The elimination method is somewhat different from the purgation method, though both serve to dissipate the pathogens. In purgation, strong drugs are used to remove drastically and rapidly substantial pathogenic factors, such as blood stasis, retention of phlegm, and fluid retention in the body, in relatively serious and acute illnesses. However, the elimination method is a moderate and less drastic process to handle pathogens that have accumulated slowly over a relatively long period of time. The digestion method is preferred when there is overeating, indigestion or malfunctioning of the stomach and spleen, and abdominal distention. The elimination method, though less radical than the purgation method, remains as a moderate *attacking* protocol. Long-term use of this method may affect the *genuine qi*. Concomitant use of tonification (see below) is recommended. Only strong subjects can tolerate repeated treatment by the elimination method.

Tonification

Tonification is the method of choice when there is a deficiency of *yin* and *yang*, *qi* and *blood*, or when there is hypofunction of a *zang-fu* organ. Proper use of tonification not only serves to restore *qi* and replenish a deficiency, but also indirectly achieves the goal of eliminating the exogenous pathogenic factors. It can reinforce and strengthen the body's natural constitution and can restore the functioning of sick cells, tissues and organs, thereby achieving the goal of therapy.

Four elements can be reinforced through tonification; they are the *qi*, *blood*, *yin* and *yang*.

1. *Replenishing the qi*: This is indicated in the presence of lassitude, weakness, easy sweating, rectal prolapse, hernia and when the pulse of a patient is ascribed to the full and deficiency types.

2. *Nourishing the blood*: This method is used when a patient is anemic, with a pale complexion, or when a patient is suffering from dizziness and vertigo, constipation or oligomenorrhea.

3. *Nourishing the yin*: This is used when a subject is emaciated, lacking in energy, irritable; suffering from palpitation, hemoptysis, anxiety, insomnia, nocturnal spontaneous ejaculation, and showing physical signs of withered skin, dry mouth and throat.

4. *Invigorating the yang*: This method is applied if a patient complains of cold aversion below the waist level, soreness and weakness of the low back and knee

joints, impotence, premature ejaculation and loose stool.

Invigorating the *qi* and *blood* is essentially accomplished through the adjuvation of the middle *jiao* because the spleen and stomach in TCM are "the sea of water and cereals" and the source of *nutrients, defensive qi, qi* and *blood*. On the other hand, *yin* and *yang* are invigorated through reinforcing the kidney and the *Mingmen*. These are the *zang* organs of *water* and *fire* from which genuine *yin* and *yang* originate.

The function of the spleen and stomach should be evaluated before starting the invigoration protocol. All the acquired nutrients have to be assimilated by the spleen and stomach. Without efficient assimilation, invigoration would fail no matter which tonic is used.

There are two ways of tonification: the fast and the slow protocols. The former method best serves patients who are extremely ill and weak and at the risk of a collapse. A good example is massive hemorrhage complicated by impending shock. The "Decoction of Radix Ginseng" should be administered. Slow tonification is more often used when the exogenous pathogen are not entirely dispelled. Under such circumstances, the *genuine qi* is still weak and deficient and the patient cannot tolerate heavy tonification drugs. Milder drug preparation such as the "Decoction of Four Noble Ingredients" is preferred. Through slow and steady invigoration, the *genuine qi* will be restored gradually.

Recent Research Concerning the Principles of Treatment

The principles of TCM treatment have gained new

physiological bases recently.

The reduction method is somewhat comparable to purgation. However, the purgation process and the drugs used in TCM are distinct from those applied in modern medicine. Conservative treatment using this method according to TCM principle has claimed a good response rate of up to 80% in acute abdomen diseases such as acute appendicitis, perforated peptic ulcers, intestinal obstructions, acute biliary infection, acute pancreatitis and ectopic pregnancy. Acute abdominal diseases may be related to obstructions in the intestines, ductal systems in the pancreas and bile duct, and the subsequent infection. According to TCM, the treatment principle of purgation is to ensure the free flow in the *zang-fu* organs so that there is no impairment of their functions. In animal experiments, TCM purgatives may stimulate intestinal peristalsis, improve blood circulation and reduce mucosal permeability. Reducing tissue edema, the luminal patency in the appendix, small bowel and the biliary pancreatic ducts and the mucosal circulation may be restored to normal physiological functioning. Rapid reabsorption of blood and body fluids in the peritoneal cavity is a positive contribution in conservative treatment of peritonitis, pancreatitis and perforated peptic ulcer. Quite a number of purgatives have antimicrobial actions. Laxative drugs such as rhubarb and magnolia bark may achieve a local antimicrobial action on the intestinal mucosa or peritoneal cavity, which promotes recovery from the inflammation of the viscera involved.

The *heat*-clearing method makes use of the *cold* nature of herbs such as Scutellaria, Coptis root, Phellodendron bark, Pittosporm root, rhizome of wind-weed, dandelion herb, viola herb, honeysuckle flower, forsythia fruit, Isatis root, wild chrysanthemum, Green Chiretta and longnoded pit viper. Quite a number of these herbs show actions against bacteria, viruses and fungi and detoxification. However, the pharmacological mechanism of the *heat*-clearing and detoxification is more than simple antimicrobial action. There is evidence that activation of the immune system bears a significant role in the pharmacology. The immune action of the herb may be even more important than the antimicrobial action. In case of Green Chiretta, its bactericidal action is weak, yet it stimulates the phagocytosis of neutrophils, activates phytoagglutinins and induces lymphocyte transformation. Thus in the treatment of pneumonia, unlike antibiotics, the antibacterial action of Green Chiretta attributes not only to its bactericidal action, but also to the active stimulation of the immune response of the host. Using the rabbit as an experimental model, after injection of endotoxin of S. typhi, *heat*-clearing drugs such as honeysuckle flower, forsythia fruit, dandelion herb and viola herb attenuate pyrexia, accelerate recovery from leucopenia and prolong the survival of the animal. Similar in vivo anti-endotoxin actions are rarely if ever found in antibiotics used in modern medicine. Only Polymyxin E carries mild anti-endotoxin action.

The tonifying method is a method of strengthening the bodily resistance and consolidating the *constitution* of the body. According to TCM, *constitution* essentially refers to two *zang-fu* organs. The kidney stores the *congenital constitution* while the spleen assimilates the *acquired constitution* for other *zang-fu* organs. In the tonifying method, herbs are used to warm the kidney *yang* and reinforce the spleen and *qi*. In brief, the tonifying method restores the function of sick cells, tissues and organs in the body through the neurohumoral and immune systems, and thereby achieves the goal of therapy. One of the traditional recipes of tonification is the Jade-Screen Powder for treating viral coryza. The essential composition of the recipe is Radix Astragali, a classical herb for reinforcing the *qi*. Experiments have elicited the antiviral action of the herb in animal studies. However, Radix Astragali does not contain interferon and does not stimulate the production of it. The herb acts on the tissues only in the presence of virus. It enhances tissue production of interferon in response to viral infection. The experimental evidence reconciles with the TCM tonification philosophy of "strengthening the body's resistance and dispelling the invading pathogenic factor".

The Practice of Prescription

In TCM practice, clinicians prescribe a combination of drugs after considering the pharmacology of the individual ingredients in the formula. Such a prescription allows drugs to be used synergistically and yet avoids negative interactions or side-effects. The art of writing a prescription depends on a basic understanding of TCM theories, particularly the theory of differentiation of syndromes. In fact, the use of prescriptions is an integral part of the TCM philosophy.

Drugs used in a prescription are often ascribed to four components of a prescription. These are the principal, adjuvant, auxiliary and the conductive ingredients. The function of these components can be understood literally. While the principal ingredient sets its goal to treat the dominant symptom complex or disease mechanism, the adjuvant potentiates the action of the principal drug. An auxiliary ingredient serves a dual purpose. Either it restrains the toxic or idiosyncratic actions of the principal drug, or it relieves minor and less serious symptoms in diseases with multiple symptom complexes. Finally, the conductive ingredient helps to convey the action of the principal drug towards the sick *zang-fu* or channel.

For example, the herb Rhizoma seu Radix Notopterygii directs drug actions to the *Taiyang* channel while the Pueraria root conducts drug actions to the *Yangming* channel. On other occasions, drugs of secondary importance may also be ascribed to this category, harmonizing or coordinating the therapeutic effects of the principal or other ingredients. In practical terms, the principal ingredient is the drug of primary importance whereas the other three ingredients are all secondary and auxiliary ones. The therapeutic effect of the recipe depends heavily on how appropriate the combination of the ingredients is.

In the example of the well-known recipe of "Decoction of Cinnamon Twigs", the principal drug is Ramulus Cinnamomi, whereas Radix Paeoniae Alba, Radix Glycyrrhizae and Rhizoma Zingiberis-Fructus Ziziphi Jujubae play the role of adjuvant, auxiliary and conductant ingredients respectively. Herba Ephedrae adds sweating action to the recipe. Used with Radix Paeoniae, it may harmonize the *defensive qi* and the *nutrient qi* to relieve the *exterior* syndrome. In coordination with Radix Aconiti Praeparata, it may restore the depleted *yang* and check perspiration. An extra load of Ramulus Cinnamomi turns the "Decoction of Cinnamom Twigs" to a prescription of easing the upward perverted flow of *qi*. This example indicates that, for the same decoction, the choice of drug combination affects significantly the therapeutic application.

Types of Preparations

In TCM, the most important forms of preparations are as follows.

Decoction

The herbs are boiled in water. Decoction is the most common form of medicine consumed for its relatively fast absorption and strong action, compared with other preparations. The ingredients in the decoction reach virtually everywhere from the *interior* to the *exterior*; and from the top to bottom of the body. Decoctions are especially suitable for treating acute illnesses for their fast action.

There are two variations of the decoction preparation. The first one is a "decoct concentrate", which is the tonic left over after long boiling of the decoction and with the herbs removed. The concentration process renders the active ingredients pure and thick enough for consumption. This procedure often finds its place in drugs for reinforcing the kidney and *qi*. When the dose of a decoction is irrelevant, it can be consumed cold or hot as an ordinary drink.

Pill

A pill contains various ground medicines glued together by pastry, honey or starch. The pill form provides the means for a sustained release of the medicine for a comparatively steady but slow absorption of the drugs. This is often used in patients who are chronically ill. Compared with decoction, pills can be easily stored for immediate use and are readily accessible in case of an emergency or acute and severe illnesses.

Powder

The powder form may be consumed orally or applied externally. Oral medicine in powder form is often used in clearing up *stagnation* in a patient. Other than for topical use, the powder form for external use also may be consumed by inhalation.

Soft Extract

The soft extract is a thick syrup form prepared by adding cane sugar or honey to the decoct concentrate for long-term oral administration in chronic ailments. The soft extract may turn sour in summer and may stay fresh longer in winter. Ointments or adhesive plasters for external application are prepared by frying the medicine in oil with yellow lead and insect wax added after the residue is discarded. It is spread on a piece of paper or cloth as paste while it is hot and is often applied to skin abscess, sores or carbuncles and to affected areas in rheumatism and *wind cold* syndromes.

Pellet

Pellets are usually made from mineral medicines. There are no fixed forms. For instance, "Treasure" pellets are small spheres. "Purple Snowy Powder", as understood literally, is in powder form, while the "Fever-Combating" pill has the shape of an ingot.

Herbal Wine

Herbal wine is prepared by immersing a variety of drugs in wine. It may be consumed orally or applied topically by rubbing. Alcohol enhances the action of the drugs through expelling *wind* pathogens and by strengthening the flow of blood. Hence herbal wine is often used to treat diseases involving numbness and pain.

Distillate

The distillate collected after decocting herbs in special pots or utensils is consumed orally as a drink. Usually distillate has a mild taste for its relatively low concentration of medicines. Hence distillates play a secondary or auxiliary role in therapy (e.g. the distillate of honeysuckle flower).

8

TRADITIONAL CHINESE HERBS

The use of natural herbs for their medicinal properties is one of the most well-known aspects of TCM in the Western world. Through centuries of research and experimentation, Chinese doctors have discovered hundreds of plants and other products that have specific therapeutic effects. It is worth noting that interest in natural remedies is on the rise in the West, with people beginning to learn about herbal medicines discovered not only in China but in other parts of the world as well. The extensive knowledge of herbs in TCM is therefore of enormous value to people everywhere, and without doubt merits further investigation. In this chapter we will give a short description of how herbs are transformed into usable drugs and explain the properties of Chinese herbs. Following that is a listing of more commonly found medicines, organized according to their functions.

The Nomenclature of Traditional Chinese Herbs

The nomenclature of traditional Chinese drugs is based

on a system with reference to the place of origin, shape, colour and other characteristics of a drug. The guidelines are briefly described in this chapter.

Nomenclature according to Place of Origin

The clinical efficacy of a herb may vary according to its place of origin, its species as well as its particular soil and cultivation. Naming herbs after their place of origin calls for attention to the notable differences between drugs produced in different localities in China. We will just quote a few examples here. *Dangshen* (Radix Codonopsis Piltosulae) is so called because it is produced in the county Shang Dang in the Shanxi Province, thus the prefix *Dang*. The prefix *Chuan* of *Chuanlian* (Rhizoma Coptidis), *Chuanbeimu* (Bulbus Fritillariae Cirrhosae), *Chuanxiong* (Rhizoma Ligustici Chuanxiong), *Chuanwu* (Radix Aconiti), *Chuanjiao* (Pericarpium Zanthoxyli) identifies the place of origin as *Chuan*, or the Sichuan Province. The prefix *Guang* of *Guangmuxiang* (Radix Saussureae Lappae) and *Guang-huoxiang* (Herba Pogostemonis) refers to Guangdong Province.

Nomenclature according to Shape

Names of drugs may be attributed to their shapes. In Chinese, Achyranithes carries the literal name of "ox knee", which the stem of the plant resembles. *Ginseng* bears the image of the human body and thus acquires the prefix of *gin* or man in Chinese before the class of drug called *seng*. Pulsatilla root got the generic name of "gray-haired old man" for the white hairy covering on the stem and leaves of the plant. Other examples are Portulaca, *longan* and Aristolochia. These names represent the generic figures they resemble, namely "horse tooth grass", "dragon eye" and "horse potato" respectively.

Nomenclature according to Natural Colour

The colour of the plant is often used in the name of the herb, or the name itself suggests a certain colour. Some examples are white atractylodes rhizome (white), natural indigo, green tangerine peel, Salvia Miltiorrhiza (green), safflower (red), rhubarb (yellow) and hematite (brown).

Nomenclature according to Flavour

The Chinese names of herbs such as Auchlandica, frankincense, musk, eagle wood, sandal wood and clove owe their names to their specific fragrance, while wild spring jujuba seed, flavescent sophora root, Asarum Sieboldii and liquorice are so named for their taste.

Nomenclature according to Biological Habitat

The prunella spike withers in summer season and has a Chinese name which means "grass withering in summer". The root tuber of Rhizoma Pinelliae ripens in mid-summer and hence acquired the name "mid-summer". Chinese ilex has the literal name of "winter green" from its leaf which remains green in winter. The herb "evergreen" is so called because its leaves remain green all year round. The Chinese names of these drugs are all named after the nature of the drug.

Nomenclature according to Therapeutic Effect

Some examples are motherwort, which is administered for gynecological diseases, while albizia flower and fleece-flower stem are administered for cases like insomnia. Buck grass is applied to relax muscles and joints. Henbane has an anesthetic effect. The seeds of the chaulmoogra tree serve to cure leprosy.

Nomenclature according to the Parts being Used

Herbs like honeysuckle flower, chrysanthemum flower, sophora flower, mulberry leaves, bamboo leaves, Cacumen Biotae, plantain seed, arcium fruit, dried tangerine or orange peel, cinnamon twigs and mulberry twigs, are so called for the part of the plant that is used as medicine. Drugs made from animals like antelope horn, rhinoceros horn, otter liver and skin of hedgehog are also named for the part being used.

Nomenclature according to the Stories and Names by which a Drug was Introduced

Cnidium fruit in Chinese literally means "fruit of the bed of a snake". The herb is so named because snakes like to hide themselves in the leaves of this plant to lay their eggs. The naming of the pharbitis seed (Semen Pharbitidis) literally as "seed of the brought-forward ox" comes from the commemoration of a thankful patient who brought an ox to the doctor as a gift after being cured with the herb. The fruit of the Rangoon creeper and the bark of Eucommia got their Chinese generic names from the name of the pioneer who first introduced the use of the drug.

The Processing of Chinese Medicine

Chinese medicines often come from herbs and raw materials which cannot be used directly without processing. Processing the drugs eliminates or attenuates their toxicity and modifies the pharmacological properties. The pharmacology of raw plants may be quite different from that of cooked herbs. Impurities or useless portions are cleared away and the medicines are also processed for storage. There are several methods of processing Chinese medicines, with each serving a different purpose.

Cleaning

There are a number of methods of cleaning drugs before storage or consumption:

1. *Washing*: This removes the soil and contaminations of the raw materials.

2. *Rinsing*: This removes the salt and stale odour of products coming from the sea or medicines preserved in salt. Sargassum, Laminaria and Cistanche are examples of herbs which require rinsing before storage and consumption.

3. *Boiling*: Materials such as Celtis Sinensis are mixed with mud. After boiling with white radish, a kind of salt is formed after cooling. The final product is much purer than the raw material.

4. *Milling*: Mineral and metallic compound medicines are often mixed with impurities. Grinding the material with water in a mortar separates the pure drug from the sediment. Cinnabar, grit, talcum, and cuttle bone are prepared using this method.

Packing and Administration

1. *Slicing or pounding*: Medicines are usually cut with knives made of various materials other than iron. Radix Rehmanniae should be cut with bamboo knives, while calamus is to be cut with copper knives. Bones and horns such as rhinoceros horn, tiger-bone, and

eaglewood are pounded to small pieces or to a powder form.

2. *Drying*: Dry drugs are easily cut and ground for storage purposes. Drying in the sun and heat-drying are often used. Light heat-drying in a warm room desiccates herbs without scorching the delicate leaves such as those of the chrysanthemum. Light roasting or curing in pots is another drying method to get rid of the moisture in the raw material. It may create a dry layer or crust which contains the product underneath. Insects such as leeches and the gadfly are dried using this curing method.

3. *Soaking:* Products such as fruit of the citron or trifoliate orange and white peony root are softened for cutting by soaking them in water. The bark of plants and nuts (almond, apricot and peach kernel) is easy to peel off after immersion in hot water.

4. *Steaming and distilling:* Poria Cocos and the bark of magnolia can easily be cut into pieces only after steaming. Volatile oils are extracted by distillation. Distillates of the honeysuckle flower and peppermint are the active ingredients used clinically.

5. *Burning and quenching:* Direct burning in fire or heating on tiles is used for shell and mineral drugs (dragon bone, oyster shell). Quenching is dipping the product in cold water or vinegar after heating over fire. Pyrite and copper ores are quenched before being smashed into small pieces. The process may also attentuate the toxicity or modify the pharmacological action of certain raw materials.

Eliminating or Reducing Toxicity and Side Effects

1. *Roasting in ashes*: Roasting the herbs, which are wrapped with paper or starch paste, removes the oil in drugs. The oil in nutmeg which causes vomiting is then removed. Fresh ginger, for example, loses its otherwise irritating side-effects after roasting and becomes more effective in warming the middle *jiao*.

2. *Stir-baking*: Baking to various degrees serves different purposes. Atractylodies Macrocephala and citron fruits (bitter orange) are lightly baked until they turn yellow. Fruit of hawthorn and malt need to be scorched, whereas oriental arborvitae and garden burnet should be charred. Pittosporm root and Squama Manitis are stir-baked to reduce their pharmacological efficacies. The side-effects of Dichroa root and Coptis root will lessen after stir-baking with wine and fresh ginger juice respectively. Aconite and dried ginger are stir-baked until smoke appears after which their toxicity is reduced to within a safe margin.

3. *Defatting*: Toxicity or a certain pharmacological action may be altered by removing the lipid content of the raw medicine. Defatting may be achieved by stir-frying as in frankincense (Resina Olibani) and myrrh (Resina Myrrhae), or by squeezing a plant wrapped in a piece of blotting paper as in the example of the croton fruit.

Changing a Herb's Properties and Increasing Its Therapeutic Effects

1. *Stir-baking with an adjuvant*: Mild stir-baking of liquorice root and astragalus root with honey enhances the functioning of the middle *jiao*. Bone and horn medicines such as tiger bone and deer horn crisply baked and layered with fat softens the products for

good absorption and potentiates their tonifying pharmacological effects. In general, wine as an adjuvant enhances the effects of certain drugs. Vinegar directs the action of drugs (e.g. nutgrass) to the liver meridian. Drugs such as pinellia, after baking with ginger juice, warm the stomach and stop vomiting. Salt directs herbs such as corktree to the kidney meridian.

2. *Fermentation:* Fermentation modifies the action of a raw medicine. After fermentation, soya bean may be used to clear exogenous pathogens. Medicated leaves are produced after the fermentation of a mixture of wheat, little red beans (Phaseolus Angularis Wight), almond and the fresh aerial parts of Artemisia Annua, Xanthium Sibiricum and Polygonum Hydropiper. Analysis of the preparation suggests that lactobacilli, volatile oils, amylase and other digestive enzymes enhance digestion, which is compatible with the TCM observation that this medicine will stimulate the functions of the spleen and stomach.

3. *Repeated steaming and drying in the sun:* The pharmacological action of a drug may be different after drying and steaming. The fresh root of rehmannia is used to clear the *internal heat* and cool the *blood* while the dry prepared rhizome is more appropriate for nourishing the *yin*. The tuber of multiflower knotweed is processed to strengthen its effects of invigorating the *yin* of the liver and kidney and the tonification of blood.

In summary, processing with heat, water and fire alone or in combination are all fundamental methods in preparing Chinese medicines.

The Properties of Chinese Drugs

The effects of Chinese medicines can be described in the context of the five flavours, four properties of drugs, as well as the theory of ascending, descending, floating and sinking.

The Five Flavours

These are described as pungent, sweet, sour, bitter, and salty. According to TCM, drugs with the same flavour share common effects on the body. It was stated in the *Nei Jing* that a pungent flavour helps to *disperse*, a sour flavour is an astringent, a sweet flavour is recuperative, a bitter flavour is consolidating and a salty flavour is softening. Therefore, it is believed that drugs with a pungent flavour are able to dissipate *heat* and exogenous pathogens as well as mobilizing the *qi*. Sour drugs may consolidate *dampness* in the body and thus may be able to improve a cough, sweating and diarrhea. Drugs sweet in taste function to help one recuperate and tonify the *yin*. Bitter drugs relieve *dampness* and purge *fire* in the body. Salty drugs have the properties of softening lumps and the stool. A plain flavour is tasteless and has the action of eliminating *dampness* and water.

The Four Properties

Drugs may be described as *cold, hot, warm* and *cool* according to their specific indications and effects on the body. Scutellaria root and coptis root eliminate *heat* and have antipyretic effects and thus they are ascribed as *cold*-natured drugs. Dried ginger and Chinese cassia bark are described as *hot*-natured drugs for their properties to warm when patients are suffering from *cold* syndromes. *Warm* and *cool* are the two intermediates between the extremes of *hot* and *cold*. Drugs that have no action on the *heat* and *cold* in the body are not included in this category.

The five flavours and the four properties of drugs are not mutually exclusive in the description of the pharmacological properties of a drug. A drug has its own flavour and property. There are a large number of different combinations of flavour and properties. Drugs of the same flavour may have different pharmacological actions and different properties. Some medicines have more than one flavour and a broader spectrum of action is expected.

Ascending, Descending, Floating and Sinking

The ascending and floating drugs direct pathogens and substances in upward and outward directions. They induce sweating, vomiting and activate the *yang qi*. On the other hand, those which direct *qi* or pathogens downward and outward are ascribed to the descending and sinking groups. They may relieve asthma, abort vomiting as well as promote purgation and diuresis.

The Combined Use of Chinese Medicines

It is unusual to use only one drug in TCM practice. The use of two or more drugs in a prescription serves to expand the clinical efficacy of an individual drug and acquire a synergic effect in the treatment of disease. It also helps to reduce or nullify the side effects of an individual drug by another one. The main theme of polypharmacy is to improve the treatment of complicated diseases.

The combined use of drugs of the same class to achieve

better therapeutic effects is called potentiation, while using two drugs of different actions or properties together is called synergism. Phellodendron bark and Anemarrhena rhizome both belong to the same class of drugs which clear the *internal heat*. Using both drugs together may more quickly restore a high body temperature to normal. Bitter apricot kernel bears a taste different from that of the pungent coltsfoot flower; yet both drugs used together may attain a better antitussive effect. On the contrary, two drugs may attenuate the toxicity or vigorous therapeutic action of each other. This phenomenon is called restraint in TCM terms and an example of this combination is the pinellia tuber and ginger. Occasionally, one drug may antagonize the action of another. Dry ginger should not be used together with scutellaria root. Sometimes two drugs are used together in order to neutralize the side effects of each other. The cold mung bean can offset the negative side effects of the croton seed when the two are used together. There are only a few drugs which are used alone, for example, the liquorice root.

Contraindications of Drugs

It is important to be familiar with the contraindications of various drugs.

Contraindication for Pregnancy

Certain drugs may induce premature labour or even cause a miscarriage. Those drugs absolutely contraindicated in pregnancy usually are toxic or strong in their therapeutic action. Croton seed, morning glory seed, thistle, poke root (Radix Phytolaccae), burreed tuber, zedoary rhizome, leech and musk are totally contraindicated in pregnancy. Drugs which restore the menstrual flow and clear away blood stasis as well as strong purgatives are also relatively contraindicated in pregnancy. Thus peach kernel, safflower, rhubarb, fruit of the immature citron, prepared aconite root and the bark of the Chinese cassia tree should be used with caution in pregnant women. Whether these relatively contraindicated drugs should be used in pregnancy depends on the clinical status of the patient. The desirable therapeutic actions and the precautions of using a drug should be well considered before its use.

Cautions of Drug Use

Some specific diet taboos are commonly practised in the Chinese tradition. It is said that pork should not be taken together with liquorice root, balloonflower root and black plum. Lilyturf root should not be cooked with crucian carp and vinegar should not be added to tuckahoe (Poria). More important for a patient is the restriction of raw material or not well-cooked food, as well as food which is difficult to digest. Foods related to skin allergies and coughs are not taken due to allergic reactions. Drugs kept at home and infested by moths and bugs can still serve a therapeutic purpose without significant loss of effect, provided the contaminated part and the contaminants are removed. However, mouldy drugs must be disposed of. Otherwise not only will the therapeutic effects be altered by the fungus but also consumption of such medicines is harmful to the patient. It would be safer to dispose of them no matter how expensive they are.

Drug Toxicity

Known poisonous drugs should also be used with great caution. Examples such as white arsenic, nux-vomica seed and datura flower carry variable levels of toxicity. Less toxic drugs, when consumed beyond a tolerable quantity, may still be extremely dangerous to a patient. An example is the cough medicine called bitter apricot seed which carries a cyanide compound. The lethal dose is about 50 to 60 pieces for an adult or 7 to 10 pieces for a child. Another example is a thyroid drug called airpotato yam. A dose of over 30 grams is toxic to the liver and may result in jaundice and abnormal liver functions.

Methods of Decoction and Taking Herbal Medicine

Traditional Chinese medicine is mostly made of raw or processed materials not ready for immediate consumption, as mentioned in the beginning of this chapter. Some form of decoction or cooking is required before use. The most common method of preparation of the medicines is to decoct or boil them in a special way to make a soup or liquid form for oral consumption. The method of decoction may dictate the action of the drug. The amount of water added, the boiling time and the cooking method vary according to the drugs being processed. For diaphoretics such as schizonepeta and peppermint stems, the active ingredients are volatile oils. In order to keep the oils unvaporized, little water should be boiled and the decoction should be quick and hot, yet short enough to leave a substantial amount of the active ingredient in the final soup. In the case of peppermint, overcooking may drive away the taste and flavour. The drug should not be added until the very end of cooking. Rhubarb is a purgative which loses its purgative effect upon lengthy boiling. On the contrary, a tonic usually requires long hours of mild boiling with adequate replenishment of water. This is how to get the full extract of the drugs in order to make the medicinal soup stronger and more effective.

Unless stated otherwise, the usual method of preparing a medicinal soup is to boil one volume of mixture of drugs in two to four volumes of water for half an hour. The final mixture is equal to about one volume of water and is used as the first run or first serving. A common practice to make full use of the medicine is to boil another two volumes of water in the mixture left behind for 15 minutes so as to get a second run for the next serving. For starchy drugs such as tuckahoe, euryl seed and Chinese yam rhizome (Rhizoma Dioscoreae), decoction should start with cold water; otherwise the starch will clump together rapidly before the active ingredients can be released. Soup accidentally overcooked until dry or charred should be disposed of. This sort of uncontrolled charring is entirely different from the programmed stir-baking of the raw drugs mentioned in an earlier section of this chapter, which serves the specific purpose of either helping the release or absorption of active ingredients from the drug. On the contrary, overcooking may destroy the active ingredient, thus rendering clinical efficacy unpredictable.

The schedule for the taking of drugs is usually at nine in the morning for the first serving and the second six hours later. An alternative method of serving is mixing the first run and second run together and divide it into two equal doses. Medicine should be given at the earliest convenience if the patient is suffering from an acute disease. Tonic medicine is usually served before meals for better drug absorption. Those suffering from pharyngitis may swallow the medicine after holding or gargling the soup in the mouth for a short while. Insomnia patients may take medicine before going to bed. Medicine should preferably be consumed on the day of preparation and should not be kept overnight without refrigeration.

SOME COMMON DRUGS IN TCM

The following list is an introduction to the common drugs used in TCM, organized according to their uses.

Diaphoretics for Treating *Exterior* Syndromes

(A) *Complex diaphoretics with pungent and warm properties*

1. *Ephedra* (Herba Ephedrae): 2.4–9 grams
   The crude drug is applicable to sweatless *wind* and *cold* syndromes. Baked ephedra is indicated for treating spasmodic coughs, asthma and lung diseases with *wind cold* or phlegm retention.

2. *Cinnamon twigs* (cassia twigs): 2.4–9 grams
   This is often used in combination with ephedra to stimulate perspiration. If a patient is sweating, it is used with a sweat astringent such as white peony root. The drug warms the meridians, dispels *wind* and *cold* pathogens, and has a mild cardiac stimulating action. Drug overdose causes palpitation.

3. *Schizonepeta* (Herba Schizonepetae): 4.5–9 grams
   This drug is best used in the early stage of invasion of *wind* and *cold*. Its diaphoretic action is milder than that of ephedra. It is also used to relieve headaches and dissipate the eruption of measles. Carbonized or charred schizonepeta stops bleeding diathesis.

4. *Ledebouriella root* (Radix Ledebouriellae): 4.5–9 grams
   The diaphoretic action of this herb is relatively slow.

Directing the *qi* upwards, it helps to relieve headaches and diarrhea. Its ability to dispel *wind* pathogens from the *interior* serves to relieve rheumatic pain in the muscles and joints.

5. *Asarum herb or wild ginger* (Herba Asari): 0.9–3 grams
   Besides having a diaphoretic action, this herb also dispels *wind cold* pathogens and phlegm. The former action is applicable to the treatment of *exterior* syndromes as well as rheumatism, while the latter is useful in cough relief.

6. *Magnolia flower* (Flos Magnoliae): 1.5–4.5 grams
   This herb contains a volatile oil which constricts the blood vessels and is indicated for the treatment of stuffy noses. Concomitant use of a pungent *cold*-natured drug is recommended when it is used to treat *wind heat* type diseases.

7. *Perilla leaf* (Folium Perillae): 4.5–9 grams
   This disperses *external wind* and *cold*, regulates the flow of vital energy, and is a mild carminative. Pathogenic reactions from eating fish or crabs may be alleviated. The stem of the plant is good for preventing miscarriage.

8. *Fresh ginger* (Rhizoma Zingiberis): 1–3 slices
   Other than the usual effects of diaphoresis and dispersion of *external wind* and *cold*, ginger warms the stomach and may stop vomiting. It is commonly used to relieve abdominal pain with *cold* present and used in patients after they have caught a cold.

9. *Chinese green onion stalk* (Caulis Allii Fistulosi or Bulbus Allii Fistulosi): 2–4 pieces
   As a diaphoretic, this also clears the meridians.

(B) *Diaphoretics with pungent and cold* properties

1. *Pueraria root or kudzuvine root* (Radix Puerariae): 4.5–
    9 grams
    This reduces the *heat* in the *exterior* compartment and
    promotes the *qi*. Experiments on animals suggest that
    the drug promotes cerebral and coronary blood flow. It
    has been used on patients with cerebral ischemia and
    angina pectoris.

2. *Peppermint* (Herba Menthae): 3–6 grams
    This drug is used, at an early stage, to relieve *wind heat*
    caused by exogenous pathogenic factors. It is often
    prescribed together with schizonepeta to achieve a
    synergistic effect. Peppermint is especially good for
    patients suffering from severe headaches and who are
    perspiring little. As peppermint contains volatile active
    ingredients, it is important to add the drug last during
    decoction.

3. *Prepared soybean* (Semen Sojae Praeparatum): 9–12
    grams
    Used in the early stages of febrile diseases, it disperses
    insidious pathogenic factors, achieving an antipyretic
    effect and relieving any fidgety feeling.

4. *Spirodela or ducksmeat* (Herba Spirodelae): 2.4–4.5
    grams
    This induces perspiration and diuresis. It is also used
    for treating urticaria and measles.

Antipyretics

(A) *Drugs of a bitter and cold nature*

1. *Chinese thorowax root* (Radix Bupleuri): 1.5–9 grams
   This is a strong antipyretic and is mainly used to treat alternate episodes of chills and fever. The effects of the drug include dispersing depressed liver energy, mobilizing stagnant *qi* and lifting the middle *jiao* energy. This drug should be used with caution in cases of asthenia of the *liver yang* and in patients with high blood pressure.

2. *Scutellaria root or baikal skullcap root* (Radix Scutellariae): 4.5–9 grams
   This is used to clear away the *heat* in the upper *jiao*. The drug is most effective in treating patients at the early stage of being affected by exogenous pathogenic factors, when there is *heat* in the lungs and a presence of yellowish thick sputum. Together with white Atractylodes rhizome, abortion and premature labour may be prevented by eliminating *heat* in the womb. When used alone, scutellaria may relieve menorrhagia due to *heat excess*.

3. *Coptis root* (Rhizoma Coptidis): 2.4–6 grams
   By clearing away *damp heat* in the middle *jiao*, acute inflammation in the digestive system (including the stomach and intestine, liver and gallbladder) may be resolved. It puts out *fire* in the heart and thus it may be used to treat aphthous ulcers and may also serve as a tranquilizer.

4. *Picrorrhiza kurrooa* (Royle ex Benth): 3–9 grams
   The effects of this drug are similar to the *damp heat* clearing and detoxifying effects of Coptis root. It is often used to treat *damp heat* in the digestive system and malnutrition in children.

5. *Phellodendron bark* (Cortex Phellodendri): 4.5–9 grams
   This clears away *heat* in the lower *jiao*, enhances the

yin and lessens any *dry* symptom complex in the body. It is also indicated for nocturnal spontaneous seminal ejaculation and hematuria.

6. *Capejasmine fruit* (Fructus Gardeniae): 4.5–9 grams
This is an antipyretic, a hemostatic as well as a sedative. It is able to clear away *heat* in the upper, middle and lower *jiaos* and may be used regardless of the *excess-deficiency* status of the patient. The side-effects of purgation cautions its use in patients suffering from diarrhea.

7. *Anemarrhena rhizome* (Rhizoma Anemarrhenae): 4.5–9 grams
This herb may relieve fever and symptoms of the *dry* category. It purges the *fire* in the stomach and kidney. It is also a strong sedative. Patients suffering from a spleen and stomach deficiency should not use this herb on a long-term basis.

8. *Chinese gentian* (Radix Gentianae): 3–9 grams
This has a specific effect of eliminating the intense *heat* or *fire* of the liver and gallbladder. A relative contra-indication of the drug is in the case of a deficiency of the spleen and stomach.

9. *Flavescent sophora root* (Radix Sophorae Flavescentis): 3–12 grams
This purges *fire* to clear the *internal heat* and relieves *dampness* through diuresis. Indications of the herb are parasitic infestation, *dampness-heat* syndromes such as dysentery, jaundice as well as skin manifestations such as pyoderma, eczema and pruritus vulva.

(B) Drugs with a sweet flavour and cold nature

1. *Gypsum* (Gypsum Fibrosum): 9–30 grams

The crude drug has a remarkable antipyretic action. By clearing the *excess heat* in the body, the gypsum achieves an antipyretic effect in cases of infectious disease such as Japanese B encephalitides, influenza and pneumonia when the fever is high, the pulse is full and the patient is delirious. The calcined preparation is applied externally to wounds for absorption of the exudate.

2. *Bamboo leaves*: 9–12 grams
   Used to clear insidious fevers and clear the *heat* of the heart, this drug helps those with difficulty in micturition as well as ulcers in the mouth and on the tongue.

3. *Trichosanthes root* (Radix Trichosanthis): 9–12 grams
   This quenches thirst (such as in patients with diabetes) and may also be used as a laxative. Recent research suggests it may be useful in inducing abortion.

4. *Reed rhizome* (Rhizoma Phragmitis): 9–15 grams
   This is used as an antipyretic for gingivitis and thirst quenching. Its effects are related to the clearing of the stomach *fire*.

5. *Mulberry leaf* (Folium Mori): 4.5–9 grams
   This removes the exogenous pathogens of *wind* and clears the *heat* in the liver and the eye. Dizziness, vertigo, conjunctivitis and other eye diseases related to *wind heat* may be treated with this herb.

6. *Chrysanthemum flower* (Flos Chrysanthemi): 4.5–9 grams
   Apart from expelling *wind* and eliminating *heat*, chrysanthemum subdues hyperactivity of the liver and hence it may be used to treat hypertension and eye diseases. Patients suffering from gastric diseases should be cautioned for drug intolerance.

(C) Drugs of a salty flavour and cold nature

1. *Root of Zhejiang figwort* (Radix Scrophulariae): 9–15 grams.
    This nourishes the *yin* to clear away any *heat*. It relieves pyogenic swellings and may be used to treat sore throats of a *yin* deficiency type.

2. *Rhinoceros horn* (Cornu Rhinoceri): 0.9–3 grams
    This has a tranquilizing effect on the mind. By clearing the *internal heat*, it is also used to treat bleeding diathesis and skin rashes related to pyrexia.

3. *Antelope horn* (Cornu Antelopis): 0.9–3 grams
    This clears the *heat* and toxic substances in the body. Delirium and seizure as complications of *wind heat* may respond to the drug.

Antitussives and Phlegm-Clearing Medicines

(A) Drugs clearing the lungs

1. *Peucedanum root or Hogfennel root* (Radix Peucedani): 4.5–9 grams
    This is used in the early stages of respiratory tract infections caused by *wind* pathogens. The *cold* nature of the drug neutralizes the *wind heat* effects of coughs and phlegm production.

2. *Arctium fruit* (Fructus Arctii): 4.5–9 grams
    The antitussive and phlegm-clearing action of this drug is related to its *cold* nature which dissipates *wind heat*. It is especially good for the treatment of a sore and

itchy throat. However, it is not indicated for patients with diarrhea.

3. *Fritillary bulb* (Bulbus Fritillariae): 4.5–9 grams
    While the Thunbergii species is good for acute coughs caused by exogenous pathogenic factors, the Cirrhosae species is primarily used to treat chronic coughs due to chronic internal consumptive disease. By nourishing the lungs, the drug clears the *fire* and phlegm in the lungs. The strong antitussive action discourages the spitting out of phlegm and thus Cirrhosae should not be used in the early stages of respiratory infection.

4. *Cicada slough* (Periostracum Cicadae): 3–6 grams
    This is used as an antitussive for coughs due to *wind heat* and it helps to relieve hoarseness of voice and laryngitis.

5. *White swallowwort* (Rhizoma Cynanchi Stauntonii): 4.5–9 grams
    This relieves coughs and reduces phlegm secretion related to stasis of the *lung qi*.

6. *Mulberry bark* (Cortex Mori Radicis): 4.5–9 grams
    For those who have *lung heat*, mulberry bark purges the *lung fire* to achieve an antitussive action. Through *zang-fu* interaction between the lung and kidney, the drug promotes diuresis to alleviate edema.

7. *Loquat leaf* (Folium Eriobotryae): 6–12 grams
    The *heat* in the lung and stomach is dissipated with the use of this herb, which relieves dyspnea, coughs as well as vomiting. The medicine should be wrapped for decocting after removing the hairy integument.

(B) Drugs warming the lungs

1. *Apricot kernel* (Semen Armeniacae Amarum): 4.5–9

grams

Bitter apricot kernel is a purgative and a mucolytic drug. It is also useful in relieving dyspnea and treating coughs ascribed to an *excess* syndrome. In contrast to the bitter apricot seed, the sweet kernel nourishes the lungs and it is good for a *deficiency* type of cough.

2. *Aster root* (Radix Asteris): 4.5–9 grams
    This is used to eliminate sputum and to treat chronic coughs due to lung asthenia. It also clears away *lung heat*.

3. *Coltsfoot flower* (Flos Farfarae): 4.5–9 grams
    This directs the *lung qi* down to relieve dyspnea. It is often used in combination with aster root.

4. *Inula flower* (Flos Inulae): 4.5–9 grams
    The Inula flower is also useful in directing the *qi* in a caudal direction. However, other than relieving dyspnea, the drug also has an antiemetic and anti-hiccough action. It should be wrapped with a piece of cloth or gauze for decocting before consumption.

(C) Expectorants

1. *Perilla seed* (Fructus Perillae): 4.5–9 grams
    This clears sputum and relieves asthma.

2. *Radish seed* (Semen Raphani): 4.5–9 grams
    Other than being used as a general expectorant, this drug invigorates the middle *jiao* and improves digestion.

3. *Pinellia tuber* (Rhizoma Pinelliae): 4.5–9 grams
    This drug is especially good at removing thin phlegm. It is also used as an antiemetic, antitussive and sedative.

4. *Platycodon root or balloon flower root* (Radix Platycodi): 2.4–6 grams
    This root relieves pain in the throat and clears away purulent sputum. It is effective in pacifying the *qi*.

(D) Antitussives

1. *Stemona root* (Radix Stemonae): 4.5–9 grams
    The pharmacological effects of this drug include nourishing the lungs and suppressing coughs. In treating coughs caused by exogenous pathogenic factors, the drug should be used together with diaphoretics which promote the *lung qi*. It is also an anthelmintic and delousing agent.

2. *Schisandra fruit or magnoliavine fruit* (Fructus Schisandrae): 1.5–4.5 grams
    An astringent with a sour taste, this is especially good for patients suffering from a *cold-deficiency* of the lung and kidney, but which have not yet been invaded by either exogenous or endogenous pathogens. The drug is indicated for excessive sweating, diarrhea and involuntary semen ejaculation.

Drugs that Regulate the Circulation of Vital Energy (Qi)

(A) Drugs for the flow of qi and elimination of stagnation

1. *Agastache or wrinkled giant hyssop* (Herba Agastachis Rugosae): 4.5–9 grams
    Qi is invigorated with this drug and the turbid *qi* is

removed. By dispersing the *internal heat*, the appetite is improved. The fresh plant is more often used in summer but a double dose is then recommended.

2. *Eupatorium Fortunei*:
    The pharmacology and dose of this drug are similar to those of Herba Agastachis Rugosae.

3. *Tangerine peel* (Pericarpium Citri Reticulatae Viride): 4.5–9 grams
    This is used as both a carminative for flatulence in the stomach as well as a mucolytic.

4. *Amomum fruit* (Fructus Amomi): 2.4–4.5 grams
    With the use of this drug, flatulence is reduced and the appetite is stimulated.

5. *Magnolia bark* (Cortex Magnoliae Officinalis): 3–9 grams
    This warms the middle *jiao* to remove the *internal damp*. Gastric distension and chest discomfort may be relieved.

6. *Round cardamom seed* (Semen Cardamomi Rotundi): 1.5–3 grams
    Just chewing the seed in one's mouth may relieve chest discomfort and stop vomiting due to a *cold deficiency* of the spleen and stomach by directing *qi* away from the upper *jiao*. The drug is not indicated in vomiting due to febrile illnesses.

7. *Eagle wood* (Lignum Aquilariae Resinatum): 0.9–3 grams
    The analgesic effect of this drug is achieved by mobilizing the stagnant *qi*. This effect is especially prominent in patients with pain of the *cold* type. Contraindication is a *yin deficiency* and hyperactivity of *fire*.

8.   *Cloves* (Flos Caryophylli): 0.9–3 grams
     Vomiting is stopped by *warming* the stomach with this
     herb. Indigestion is improved. The drug is often used
     together with kaki calyx in treating hiccups in *cold
     deficiency* diseases.

(B) Drugs relieving stagnancy of qi and pain

1.   *Cyperus tuber or flatsedge tuber* (Rhizoma Cyperi): 4.5–
     9 grams
     This mobilizes the stagnant *qi* and exerts an anti-
     spasmodic action on smooth muscles. It is often used to
     treat dysmenorrhea and menstrual disorders.

2.   *Curcuma root* (Radix Curcumae): 4.5–9 grams
     This drug invigorates stagnation of the *qi* and *blood* in
     the chest to alleviate chest pain.

3.   *Lindera root* (Radix Linderae): 3–9 grams
     Pain relief is essentially focused on the epigastrium
     and the abdomen through dispersing *cold* and stagnant
     qi.

4.   *Aucklandia root* (Radix Aucklandiae): 3–6 grams
     The roasted root stops diarrhea and reduces abdominal
     pain.

(C) Drugs that disintegrate aggregated and stagnated qi

1.   *Immature bitter orange* (Fructus Aurantii Immaturus):
     2.4–4.05 grams
     This disperses stagnated *qi* and promotes excretion of
     food stagnant in the gastrointestinal tract. Abdominal
     distension, flatulence and chest discomfort are relieved.
     Patients suffering from a *deficiency* syndrome should
     avoid consuming this drug.

2. *Green tangerine peel* (Pericarpium Citri Reticulatae Viridae): 2.5–4.5 grams
    The effect of this drug is similar to but milder than that of immature bitter orange and is often used to treat thoracic pain.

Drugs for Regulating the Blood

(A) *Drugs for eliminating pathological heat from the blood*

1. *Rehmannia root* (Radix Rehmanniae): 9–15 grams
    By nourishing the *yin*, pathological *heat* in the blood is removed and production of body fluids is restored or stimulated. The *heat*-clearing action of the raw plant is even stronger than the dried one.

2. *Moutan bark* (Cortex Moutan Radicis): 4.5–9 grams
    This is used to cool *blood heat*, clear insidious *fire*, as well as to regulate menstrual flow in amenorrhea and remove blood stasis.

3. *Purple gromwell root* (Radix Arnebiae seu Lithospermi): 4.5–9 grams
    This root cools the blood, lowers a high body temperature and relieves rashes in febrile illnesses. It also has a detoxifying action.

4. *Imperata rhizome or cogon-grass rhizome* (Rhizoma Imperatae): 3–9 grams
    The dry rhizome cools the blood and stops bleeding. It may be used as a diuretic and as a detoxification drug. The cogon flower is used to stop epistaxis.

5. *Pulsatilla root* (Radix Pulsatillae): 9–15 grams
   This drug is used to treat dysentery complicated with fever, such as amoebic dysentery.

6. *Wolfberry bark* (Cortex Lycii Radicis): 4.5–9 grams
   As a drug that treats sweating and long-term fever, it is often used to treat tuberculosis.

(B) Hemostatic Drugs

1. *Biota tops* (Cacumen Biotae): 4.5–9 grams
   Damp heat is removed from the blood with this drug. It is used to treat hemoptysis.

2. *Bletilla tuber* (Rhizoma Bletillae): 4.5–9 grams
   This may be used to treat both hemoptysis and hematemesis.

3. *Sanguisorba root or burnet root* (Radix Sanguisorbae): 4.5–9 grams
   This eliminates *damp heat* from the blood and is useful in treating gastrointestinal bleeding.

4. *Sophora flower bud* (Flos Sophorae): 9–15 grams
   The coolant effect is especially good for a bleeding hemorrhoid and purpura.

5. *Small thistle* (Herba Cephalanoploris): 9–30 grams
   This is used to stop bleeding and absorb clots in various types of hemorrhagic diseases.

6. *Notoginseng* (Radix Notoginseng): 3–9 grams
   The drug may be indicated in various types of bleeding. It stops bleeding and is able to help resolution of ecchymosis and pain. The preferred way of consumption is to swallow the drug in powder form.

7. *Chinese mugwort leaf* (Folium Artemisiae Argyi): 3–9 grams

By warming the middle *jiao* and regulating *qi*, this herb stops bleeding and regulates menstruation.

8. *Motherwort* (Herba Leonuri): 9–15 grams
    This has a dual action of dissipating blood stasis and stimulating the regulatory power of the body. In case of postpartum bleeding and abdominal pain, the drug relieves symptoms by invigorating blood and restoring the homeostasis of the meridians. The seed, Semen Leonuri, may relieve conjunctivitis, in addition to having similar pharmacological effects as motherwort.

(C) Drugs for invigorating blood circulation and eliminating blood stasis

1. *Corydalis tuber* (Rhizoma Corydalis): 4.5–9 grams
    The mechanism of this analgesia is to activate *qi* and promote blood circulation. It is thus often used to relieve pain due to stagnation of both blood and *qi*.

2. *Cat-tail pollen* (Pollen Typhae): 6–9 grams
    The raw preparation of this herb promotes blood circulation and relieves stasis. Its pharmacological property is changed from mild to astringent after stir-baking to a charred colour and may be used as a general hemostatic.

3. *Chuanxiong rhizome* (Rhizoma Ligustici Chuanxiong): 4.5–15 grams
    This is another drug for invigorating blood circulation and the flow of *qi*. It may be used to treat menstrual disorders. According to TCM, the pharmacological action of this rhizome is focused on the cephalic side and is able to dissipate stagnant *qi*. Thus it is often used to treat headaches (migraine or other types) ascribed to a failure of cephalic rise of lucid *yang* and chest pain due to stagnant *liver qi*. Contraindications of

its use are concomitant *blood deficiency* and hyper-activity of *liver yang* as well as menorrhagia.

4. *Red peony root* (Radix Paeoniae Rubra): 4.5–9 grams
   This drug disperses stasis, invigorates blood and clears away *heat*, and is often used when there is liver derangement.

5. *Red sage root* (Radix Salviae Miltiorrhizae): 4.5–9 grams
   This herb has a mild blood nourishing effect and a strong invigorating action. The most important use of the drug is in treating coronary heart disease.

6. *Safflower* (Flos Carthami): 2.4–4.5 grams
   This is used to promote blood circulation, relieve stasis, and promote tissue regeneration. Bleeding diathesis is a contraindication.

7. *Zedoary* (Rhizoma Zedoariae): 4.5–9 grams
   This is more effective in promoting qi circulation than in removing blood stasis. It is often used for hypochondriac pain due to depressed *qi* and to disintegrate tumors such as carcinoma of the cervix.

8. *Bugleweed* (Herba Lycopi): 6–9 grams
   This mobilizes stagnant blood in oligomenorrhea or amenorrhea. It is also used for relieving postpartum abdominal pain and symptoms related to blood stasis. This drug also reduces edema through diuresis.

9. *Peach kernel* (Semen Persicae): 4.5–9 grams
   This activates stagnant blood, removes clots in the body and resolves ecchymoses after a contusion or external injury. It is also good for constipation.

10. *Faeces of the flying squirrel* (Faeces Trogopterorum): 3–9 grams

This is very effective in relieving blood stasis and in alleviating pain. Cat-tail pollen potentiates its therapeutic effect of alleviating muscle spasm. By relieving blood stasis, menstrual flow is restored in patients with amenorrhea.

11. *Leech* (Hirudo Nipponica): 0.9–1.5 grams
This has a strong effect of activating stagnant blood.

Diuretics

1. *Poria* (Tuckahoe): 9–15 grams
This drug invigorates the spleen by eliminating dampness. Its sedative action is attributed to its nourishing effect on the heart. The red poria should be used instead when *damp-heat* is predominant in the body.

2. *Umbellate pore fungus* (Polyporus Umbellatus): 6–12 grams
The diuretic action of this drug is stronger than that of poria. Contrary to poria, this drug does not invigorate the spleen. Polysaccharides extracted from the herb have been found to have an effect against cancer.

3. *Water-plantain tuber* (Rhizoma Alismatis): 9–15 grams
The diuretic and *dampness* eliminating actions serve the dual purpose of reducing fluid retention and edema. It is also used to expel *heat* in the body.

4. *Plantain seed* (Semen Plantaginis): 9–15 grams
This induces diuresis, dissipates *heat* and has an antimicrobial action. It is indicated in oliguria, fluid retention and diarrhea.

5. *Clematis stem* (Clematidis Armandii): 3–12 grams
   The diuretic and *heat* dissipating actions make this drug useful in eliminating *damp heat* in the body. Thus it is used in the treatment of dysuria and gonorrhea. It can also be used to promote lactation.

6. *Talc* (Talcum): 9–12 grams
   This drug has the characteristic action of eliminating *summer heat*. It also stimulates milk production and diuresis.

7. *Seven-lobed yam* (Rhizoma Dioscoreae Septemlobae): 9–12 grams
   This separates the *refined substances* from *turbidity* in the body fluids and eliminates the latter from the body. Frequency and pyuria attributed to *damp heat* may be relieved. The drug is also useful in the treatment of *dampness*-related diseases such as rheumatism and muscle pains.

Purgatives

(A) *Drugs of a cold nature for loosening the bowels*

1. *Rhubarb* (Radix et Rhizoma Rhei): 4.5–9 grams
   Stagnant and undigested food in the alimentary canal are purged with the use of rhubarb. The raw herb is used to clear *heat* symptoms caused by excessive pathogenic factors. The fabricated preparation is generally used to correct blood stasis and to induce menstruation in amenorrhea. The powder form taken before sleep at a dose of 1.5 g is used as a purgative.

2. *Mirabilite or Glauber's salt or sodium sulphate* (Natrii Sulfas): 3–9 grams

This herb is a stool softener. It also dissipates *heat* and stagnancy in the gut. Its purgative action is very strong when the herb is used together with raw rhubarb.

(B) *Drugs of a warm nature for loosening the bowels*

Croton seed (Semen Crotonis): 0.003 to 0.3 gram
Croton Seed cream should only be used after undergoing a degreasing process which gets rid of its poison. Only a very small amount of the drug is strongly effective in purgation and diuresis. The strong phlegm dissipation action is achieved through purgation of accumulated *cold* in the *zang-fu*. In TCM, when acute abdomen pain is attributed to phlegm stagnation, this herb may be used for relief.

(C) *Diuretics and hydrogogues*

1. *Peking spurge root* (Euphorbia Pekinensis): 0.6–1.5 grams
    This is consumed in powder form. Fluid retention in patients with edema, pleural effusion and ascites may be treated with this herb.

2. *Kansui root* (Radix Euphorbiae Kansui): 0.6–1.5 grams
    The dosage and effects of this herb are similar to those of the Peking spurge root.

(D) *Laxatives*

1. *Hemp seed* (Fructus Cannabis): 6–12 grams
    This laxative lubricates the bowel and keeps the stool moist. It is often used on the elderly and on patients whose *blood* and *fluid* are depleted.

2. *Honey* (Mel): 9–30 grams
    As a lubricant and stool softener, honey also reinforces the functioning of the middle *jiao*.

(E) Digestives and evacuants

1. *Medicated leaven* (Massa Fermentata Medicinalis): 6–9 grams
   This herbal mixture reinforces the functioning of the spleen and stomach. Appetite is improved through alleviating food stagnancy. The charred preparation stops diarrhea.

2. *Hawthorn fruit* (Fructus Crataegi): 6–9 grams
   This is particularly effective in removing food stasis due to fat and meat. It helps to disperse blood stasis in dysmenorrhea, coronary heart disease and trauma.

3. *Germinated millet* (Fructus Setariae Germinatus) *and germinated barley* (Fructus Hordei Germinatus): each 6–9 grams
   This drug is most effective against dyspepsia and indigestion due to rice and cereal. After stir-baking and decocting, 60 grams of the preparation helps to interrupt lactation.

4. *Chicken's gizzard-skin* (Endothelium Corneum Gigeriae Galli): 6–9 grams
   This is used to eliminate indigestion, to disperse blood stasis and to dispel calculi in the urinary and biliary tracts.

The above digestives and evacuants are seldom used alone. They are usually prescribed in combination with drugs of the same or other classes.

Drugs for Softening Hard Lumps

1. *Seaweed or sargassum* (Sargassum Pallidum): 9–15

grams

In TCM, this herb has the effect of softening hard lumps and mobilizing stagnant fluids. Sargassum is rich in iodine, which is useful for treating endemic goitres and for mucolytic action in bronchitis. It is also indicated in lymphadenitis.

2. *Laminaria* (Thallus Laminariae): 9–15 grams
The clinical use and dosage of this are similar to those of sargassum.

3. *Prunella spike or selfheal spike* (Spica Prunellae): 9–15 grams
This is used to clear up *heat* in the liver and may be used in tuberculous lymphadenitis.

4. *Turtle shell* (Carapax Trionycis): 15–30 grams
Used as an antipyretic, this herb works by invigorating the *yin*. Hepatomegaly and splenomegaly, especially in the case of malaria, may be dissolved due to the herb's softening action.

Drugs for Resolving Dampness

1. *Atractylodes rhizome* (Rhizoma Atractylodis): 4.5–9 grams
The rhizome keeps *dampness* away and invigorates the spleen. The rich ingredients found in it such as vitamin A and vitamin D are effective against night blindness, rickets and keratosis.

2. *Oriental wormwood* (Herba Artemisiae Scopariae): 9–15 grams
This drug clears *damp* pathogens from the lower *jiao*

and acts especially on the liver and the gallbladder and hence it is commonly used to clear up jaundice in a patient.

3. *Tetranda root* (Radix Stephaniae Tetrandrae): 4.5–9 grams
    This also eliminates *dampness* and has an antipyretic action. It may also be used to treat rheumatism and myalgia.

4. *Coix seed or Job's tears seed* (Semen Coicis): 9–15 grams
    This is used to improve the functioning of the spleen, to dispel *dampness*, and to clear away pus.

Analgesics and Wind Expellants

1. *Notopterygium root* (Rhizoma seu Radix Notopterygii): 4.5–9 grams
    This root is antirheumatic and analgesic. Its pharmacological actions also include inducing perspiration in order to dispel exogenous pathogenic factors.

2. *Pubescent angelica root* (Radix Angelicae Pubescentis): 4.5–9 grams
    This is used to expel *wind* and remove *dampness*. Its indications are rheumatic and muscle pains.

3. *Large-leaf gentian root* (Radix Gentianae Macrophyllae): 4.5–9 grams
    The antirheumatic actions of this root are attributed to the expulsion of *wind* pathogens, the regulation of blood and the relaxation of the tendons.

4. *Chaenomeles fruit or flowering-quince fruit* (Fructus Chaenomelis): 4.5–9 grams
    This fruit is used to relax the tendons, alleviate muscle spasms and nourish the liver.

5. *Achyranthes root* (Radix Achyranthis Bidentatae): 4.5–9 grams
    The Achyranthes root drains *qi* to the channels in the lower part of the body. Hence it is used to treat asthenia of the lower limbs and oligomenorrhea, as well as to induce diuresis.

Astringents and Hemostatics

(A) Astringent drugs to interrupt seminal emissions

1. *Dogwood fruit* (Fructus Corni): 4.5–9 grams
    This fruit replenishes the essences of the liver and kidney. The indications of the drug are for spontaneous seminal emission, oversweating and urinary frequency due to a *cold deficiency*. The drug is contraindicated for patients with flaring up of *fire* from the *Mingmen* meridian or for subjects suffering from a *damp-heat* syndrome.

2. *Mantis egg-case* (Ootheca Mantidis): 4.5–9 grams
    The egg case reinforces the *kidney yang* and helps to relieve urinary frequency and incontinence, premature seminal ejaculation as well as enuresis due to a *kidney yang* deficiency.

3. *Euryale seed* (Semen Euryales): 9–30 grams
    This is used for the treatment of spermatorrhea and nocturnal or premature seminal ejaculation. Another

indication is for stopping diarrhea through nourishing the spleen.

4. *Raspberry fruit* (Fructus Rubi): 4.5–9 grams
   This is used as an astringent to invigorate the kidney and to treat nocturia.

5. *Oyster shell* (Concha Ostreae Usta): 15–30 grams
   This is not only an astringent for the treatment of seminal emission and spermatorrhea, but also a softener for hard lumps. The crude drug nourishes the *yin* to suppress the *yang*. The ignited oyster shell is good for treating night sweating.

(B) Astringent drugs to stop diarrhea

1. *Chebula fruit* (Fructus Chebulae): 4.5–9 grams
   This astringent has a remarkable anti-diarrhetic effect.

2. *Red halloysite* (Halloysitum Rubrum): 9–15 grams
   This drug is indicated in a *deficiency* syndrome such as chronic diarrhea and dysentery. It also helps to stop bleeding.

3. *Limonite* (Limonitum): 9–15 grams
   The dosage and therapeutic effects of this drug are the same as that of red halloysite.

4. *Black plum or mume* (Fructus Mume): 3–9 grams
   Other than being used for stopping chronic diarrhea, this drug also has an astringent effect on the lungs to stop coughing. It stimulates the production of *fluids* for quenching thirst. It is also used as an anthelmintic against ascariasis.

5. *Poppy capsule* (Pericarpium Papaveris): 4.5–9 grams
   The rich content of morphine in the opium poppy capsule serves effectively to relieve diarrhea and

coughs. The astringent property of this drug is also effective for sweating and spermatorrhea. It is contraindicated for patients with exogenous pathogenic factors or internal pathogenic *fire*.

(C) Antihydrotics

Ephedra root (Radix Ephedrae): 3–9 grams
This is used as an anhydrotic agent for the treatment of spontaneous perspiration and night sweats. The specific therapeutic action depends on the auxiliary drugs used.

Sedatives and Tranquilizers

(A) Mineral drugs

1. *Amber* (Succinum): 0.9–3 grams
    Sedation is achieved by subduing the hyperactivity of the liver.
    It also promotes diuresis, disperses stagnation and stops hematuria.

2. *Magnetite* (Magnetitum): 9–30 grams
    This drug can be used to subdue the exuberance of the *liver yang* and boost the waning or *deficiency* of the kidney. As a sedative, this drug is effective against dizziness and insomnia.

3. *Sea-ear shell or abalone shell* (Concha Haliotidis): 9–30 grams
    This clears the internal heat by subduing the hyperactivity of the *liver yang*. Vertigo, dizziness or conjunctival diseases due to *liver fire* may also be treated with the shell.

4. *Cinnabar* (Cinnabaris): 0.3–0.9 grams
    This has been used for a long time in TCM as a sedative. It acts on the heart and may neutralize any poisonous pathogens in the *zang-fu*. Cinnabar contains mercurial compounds and should be used sparingly in order to avoid toxicity.

5. *Dragon's bone* (Os Draconis): 9–15 grams
    Its function is equivalent to that of magnetite. The calcined drug can be used to arrest discharges and check profuse sweating.

6. *Ignited yellow earth* (Terra Flava Usta): 9–30 grams
    This stops nausea, vomiting, hemetemesis and bleeding via the rectum. Diarrhea due to a *yang deficiency* of the spleen and stomach may also be relieved. This drug must be wrapped for decoction before consumption.

7. *Red Ochre* (Ochra): 9–15 grams
    This drug is effective against nausea, vomiting, aerophagia and discomfort in the abdomen due to belching.

(B) Non-mineral drugs

1. *Wild (spiny) jujuba seed* (Semen Ziziphi Spinosae): 6–12 grams
    The actions of this herb are on the heart. It has an antidepressant action. As a hypnotic, the drug may be consumed in powder form at a dose of 3 grams before retiring.

2. *Polygala root* (Radix Polygalae): 2.4–6 grams
    This is a sedative for neurasthenia and eliminates phlegm.

3. *Arborvitae seed* (Semen Biotae): 4.5–9 grams
    This is not only a sedative, but also a lubricant

purgative for constipation.

(C) *Anticonvulsants*

1. *Scorpion* (Scorpio): 0.9–1.5 grams
    This subdues the endogenous *wind* and hence may be used as an anticonvulsant. The tail piece of the scorpion is said to be effective in this treatment.

2. *Gastrodia tuber* (Rhizoma Gastrodiae): 4.5–9 grams
    Being able to subdue *wind* pathogens, this herb is particularly effective in relieving dizziness and vertigo.

3. *Uncaria stem with hooks* (Ramulus Uncariae cum Uncis): 4.5–9 grams
    This herb subdues endogenous *wind* and *heat* as well as hyperactivity of the liver. Dizziness, vertigo and giddiness or headache due to hyperactivity of the *liver yang* may be treated with this. Lengthy decoction destroys the active properties of the herb, therefore it is best to add the herb just before the end of decoction to preserve its clinical efficacy.

Aromatic Stimulants

1. *Storax or Styrax* (Styrax Liguidus): 0.3–0.9 grams
    This drug clears *wind-phlegm* which accumulates in the body and causes cerebrovascular accident. Loss of consciousness or dementia may be cured more quickly with this medicine.

2. *Ox gallstone* (Calculus Bovis): 0.3–1.5 grams
    The gallstone of an ox is indicated for loss of consciousness or delirium during acute febrile illnesses.

3. *Grass-leaved sweetflag rhizome* (Rhizoma Acori Graminei): 3–9 grams
   This herb is used when there is a loss of consciousness or delirium caused by phlegm.

4. *Musk* (Moschus): 0.03–0.15 grams
   This is a central nervous system stimulant for all kinds of coma or delirium. Owing to its high penetrating power, the drug is often used topically in plaster form with other ingredients. Its effects of relieving pain and swelling are often quite remarkable. Musk should never be decocted but should only be consumed in the form of a pellet or powder.

Tonics

(A) *Drugs for replenishing the qi*

1. *Ginseng* (Radix Ginseng): 1.5–6 grams
   This is used to replenish the *qi* and to promote the secretion of body fluids. Ginseng has the effect of reinforcing the *genuine qi* of the *zang-fu* organs. Used with Chinese angelica root, it has a synergistic action in *blood* nourishing. When it is used with prepared aconite root, *yang* is reinforced. Whenever there is *deficiency* in a *zang-fu* organ, ginseng has the ability of conducting another drug to its target *zang-fu* organ, thereby increasing its efficacy. Ginseng may be used in all *deficiency* syndromes regardless of the *heat* and *cold* nature of the ailment. While white ginseng is generally used, red ginseng is characterized by a sweet flavour and warm nature and is able to replenish the *yang qi*. The relatively *cold* pharmacological nature of

American ginseng serves to nourish the *yin* and to clear away *fire* in the *zang-fu* organs.

2. *Pilose Asiabell root* (Radix Codonopsis Pilosulae): 3–12 grams
    This strengthens the middle *jiao* and *qi*. However the replenishing effects are not so strong as those of ginseng.

3. *Astragalus root* (Radix Astragali): 9–30 grams
    The action of this root is to reinforce *qi* and to replenish any *deficiency* in the *zang-fu* organs. The raw herb consolidates resistance of the *exterior* against external pathogens and has a healing effect on abscesses and superficial wounds. The ignited drug acts on the middle *jiao* to stimulate the *qi*, while the epidermis induces diuresis and expels *dampness* in the body.

4. *White atractylodes rhizome* (Rhizoma Atractylodis Macrocephalae): 6–12 grams
    This is used to replenish a *deficiency* of the spleen. The rhizome is thus useful in promoting the assimilation function of the spleen and in eliminating *dampness*. A loose watery stool may become normal again through this process.

5. *Chinese yam* (Rhizoma Dioscoreae): 9–15 grams
    This herb tonifies the spleen and eliminates *dampness*. Its anti-diarrheal action is quite good in diseases attributable to a *deficiency* of the spleen. Another action of the drug is the invigoration of the kidney and in checking spermatorrhea. The dual action of the Chinese yam warrants its use in diseases which involve a *deficiency* of both the spleen and the kidney.

6. *Liquorice or licorice root* (Radix Glycyrrhizae): 2.4–6 grams
    Bearing an antispasmodic action and a pharmacological action similar to that of glucuronate, this herb is used as an ingredient in detoxification. It is also used for treating boils as well as relieving symptoms of food poisoning and ulcer pain. The drug, after being processed by the ignition method, is capable of strengthening the functions of the middle *jiao* and *qi*.

7. *Jujube or Chinese date* (Frucuts Ziziphi Jujubae): 3–10 pieces
    This is used to regulate the vital functions of the stomach, to promote the production of body fluids, and to support the *genuine qi*. With fresh ginger, it harmonizes *defensive energy, vital energy,* nutrients and blood.

(B) Blood tonics or drugs for nourishing the blood

1. *Prepared rehmannia root* (Radix Rehmanniae Prae-parata) : 9–15 grams
    This replenishes the *vital qi* and *blood*, and nourishes the *kidney yin*. A side-effect of the drug is indigestion and hence it should not be used on patients with anorexia and diarrhea.

2. *Fleeceflower root* (Radix Polygoni Multiflori): 9–15 grams
    The therapeutic effects of this root are quite similar to, but not as strong as, those of the prepared rehmannia root. The prepared drug replenishes the *vital qi* of the liver and kidney and is indicated for insomnia and for preventing gray hair. In contrast to the rehmannia root, fleeceflower does not affect the functions of the spleen and stomach. In fact, the raw drug may be used

to treat constipation and is also effective in treating boils. Its vine, fleeceflower vine, is effective against insomnia due to emotional upset.

3. *Chinese angelica root* (Radix Angelicae Sinensis): 6–12 grams
This nourishes the blood and invigorates its circulation. It is an important ingredient in the treatment of menstrual disorders. The pharmacological action of the herb varies according to the parts of the plant. The body of the plant replenishes the blood and purges the gut in patients with constipation, while the tail part eradicates blood stasis and invigorates blood circulation. Owing to its strong invigorating effect on the blood, the Chinese angelica root should not be used alone on patients with menorrhagia or bleeding diatheses. In animal experiments on rabbits, dogs and guinea pigs, the extract of the angelica root has induced uterine contraction but has also relaxed a sustained contraction of the uterus.

4. *White peony root* (Radix Paeoniae Alba): 6–9 grams
This is an astringent for the *yin* and blood. It nourishes the blood and relieves abdominal colic when used in combination with Chinese angelica root and liquorice root respectively. With cassia twigs, any *exterior deficiency* is replenished and spontaneous perspiration is checked.

5. *Donkey-hide gelatin or ass-hide glue* (Colla Corii Asini): 6–9 grams
Both the *yin* and the blood are nourished by this drug to arrest bleeding diathesis. The gelatin moistens the lungs to relieve phlegm. Owing to its possible side-effect on the stomach, the dose of gelatin used should be appropriately reduced for patients with gastric disorders.

(C) Yin-replenishing drugs

1. *Glehnia root* (Radix Glehniae): 6–9 grams
    This root dissipates *heat* and replenishes the *essence* of the lungs. The ladybell root species eliminates phlegm to relieve coughs. The drug is not indicated when a *wind* pathogen prevails in a patient.

2. *Ophiopogon root or lilyturf root* (Radix Ophiopogonis): 6–9 grams
    This is used to nourish the *yin* of the lung and stomach, as well as to clear away the *fire* in the *zang-fu* organs. It should be noted that this drug should not be used at the early stages of an *exterior* syndrome attributable to *wind* pathogens.

3. *Dendrobium* (Herba Dendrobii): 6–12 grams
    The *yin* of the stomach is nourished with this drug and the *heat* may thus be cleared away. Together with dried reed rhizome (Rhizoma Phragmitis), this herb can cure oral ulcers and gingivitis.

4. *Lucid ligustrum fruit or glossy privet fruit* (Fructus Ligustri Lucidi): 4.5–9 grams
    This is used to replenish the *essence* of the liver and kidney and to improve eyesight.

5. *Tortoise plastron* (Plastrum Testudinis): 15–30 grams
    This subdues an excess of *yang* by nourishing the *yin*. *Heat* symptoms due to flaring up of the asthenic *fire* are relieved. The medicine also helps to strengthen the back and lower limbs.

(D) Drugs for dispelling internal cold

1. *Prepared aconite root* (Radix Aconiti Praeparata): 3–9 grams
    As a cardiotonic, this warms the *yang* and dispels *cold*.

It also restores the *essential yang* of the spleen and kidney. A tonic formula is more effective if aconite is added as an ingredient.

2. *Cinnamon bark or cassia bark* (Cortex Cinnamomi): 1.5 –6 grams
    The *warm heat* nature of this drug reinforces the *yang* and replenishes the *fire* from the *Mingmen*. Prepared aconite root can be used for treating both acute and chronic diseases, while cinnamon bark is more suitable for chronic diseases. Hence cinnamon is less effective than prepared aconite root in restoring *yang* from a collapse or restoring the vital function in a patient in shock. Cinnamon is contraindicated in pregnancy as well as for patients with a deficiency of *yin* and a hyperactivity of *yang*, sore throat and bleeding diathesis.

3. *Dried ginger* (Rhizoma Zingiberis): 3–9 grams
    This herb is used to warm the middle *jiao* (stomach) by dispersing *cold*. The prepared drug is also used to warm the lower *jiao* (intestines) to stop abdominal pain and diarrhea due to *cold* pathogens.

4. *Evodia fruit* (Fructus Evodiae): 3–6 grams
    This fruit is used to dispel *cold* by warming the middle *jiao*. Pain is relieved through restoring the correct direction of flow of the *qi*. Hence it may be used to treat *cold*-related pain in the stomach and abdomen and for hernia. The drug should be used with caution in pregnancy.

(E) *Drugs for reinforcing the vital functions*

1. *Dodder seed* (Semen Cuscutae): 6–12 grams
    This drug is used to nourish the liver and kidney. The seed is most commonly used in *yang-deficient* ailments

such as spontaneous seminal emission, impotence and hesitant urination.

2. *Flattened milkvetch seed* (Semen Astragali Complanati): 4.5–9 grams
   This is used to reinforce the *yang* and kidney in patients being treated for low back pain, knee discomforts due to cold, impotence and premature seminal ejaculation. The herb is also well known for treating morning diarrhea and illnesses related to a *cold deficiency* of the kidney and spleen.

3. *Morinda root* (Radix Morindae Officinalis): 4.5–9 grams
   This root reinforces the vital functions of the *kidney yang* and dispels *wind* pathogens and *dampness* from the body.

4. *Human placenta* (Placenta Hominis): 3–9 grams
   The dried organ nourishes the *essence* of the kidney and the body. It is known to be particularly good for strengthening one's *congenital qi*.

5. *Cistanche* (Herba Cistanchis): 6–12 grams
   This is used to reinforce the *kidney yang* for the treatment of impotence and premature ejaculation. It is also used as a mild laxative for chronic constipation.

6. *Eucommia bark* (Cortex Eucommiae): 9–12 grams
   This plant nourishes the liver and kidney. Strengthening the tendons and bones, it is often used to relieve lumbago and weakness in the lower limbs.

7. *Dipsacus root or teasel root* (Radix Dipsaci): 6–12 grams
   Other than nourishing the liver and kidney and strengthening the tendons and bones, this medicine also promotes the healing of traumatic wounds.

8. *Pilose antler or pilose deerhorn* (Cornu Cervi Pantotrichum): 0.3–0.9 gram

This drug comes from the hairy antler of a young male deer. It reinforces the *essence* and marrow and strongly promotes the *original vital functions* or the *original yang*. Despite its inferior effectiveness, the ossified horn is a common and less expensive substitute of pilose antler. The glue form of the antler after decoction and stewing serves both tonification and hemostatic purposes. The residue left behind after decoction and stewing is called deglued antler powder, which has a similar but less potent action.

Detoxifying Drugs

1. *Honeysuckle flower* (Flos Lonicerae): 9–15 grams

This dissipates *internal heat* and clears the *internal fire* in the *zang-fu* organs. It is also used to resolve swelling and edema by its detoxification action. The distillate of the honeysuckle flower has a relatively mild flavour and weak effect. In the hot summer, it is used in the prevention and treatment of boils and furuncles in children.

2. *Forsythia fruit* (Fructus Forsythiae): 9–15 grams

The pharmacological action of this is similar to that of the honeysuckle flower. Both the forsythia fruit and honeysuckle flower are important medicines for treating boils and furuncles.

3. *Subprostrate sophora root* (Radix Sophorae Subprostratae): 3–9 grams

This herb is used to purge the excess *fire* and detoxify

the *zang-fu*. It is often used in the treatment of sore throats.

4.   *Coating of the mung bean*: 1.5–9 grams
     The bean coating is used in detoxification for arsenic and metal poisoning.

Anthelmintics

1.   *Areca seed or betel nut* (Semen Arecae): 3–15 grams
     This stimulates the appetite and relieves constipation due to food indigestion. A decoction of 30-90 grams of areca seed may be used to treat cestodiasis and fascioliasis. The coating is called areca peel, which is a diuretic and carminative used for eliminating *dampness*. It relaxes the middle *jiao* by halting the perverted upward flow of *qi*. Ascites and edema may be relieved through diuresis.

2.   *Quisqualis fruit or Rangoon creeper fruit* (Fructus Quisqualis): 3–9 grams
     This is primarily an anthelmintic often consumed after stir-baking. After use, one's appetite and digestion usually return to normal. This is a drug commonly used against ascariasis.

3.   *Stemona root* (Radix Stemonae): 4.5–9 grams
     This is used as anthelmintic to treat ascariasis, enterobiasis and louse infestation. Its antitussive action justifies its use in acute or chronic bronchitis and tuberculosis.

4.   *Dichroa root* (Radix Dichroae): 4.5–9 grams
     This is used to treat malaria and induce vomiting.

9

ACUPUNCTURE AND MOXIBUSTION

Acupuncture and moxibustion therapy is a method of healing through stimulating the acupoints along the meridians and collaterals by needles and moxa sticks (rolls made of moxa). This treatment method, according to TCM, restores the free flow and harmony of *qi* and *blood* which are essential for good health and for recovery from disease.

Meridians

The concept of meridians is fundamental in TCM and must be clearly understood in order to comprehend both Chinese medicine in general and acupuncture in particular. Meridians are one of China's most unique discoveries regarding the human body, and have been basically unknown to the Western world until recent times, when acupuncture has come to the attention of both laymen and doctors in many countries. Without profound knowledge of and research into the meridians, the science of acupuncture could not exist.

Meridians are channels within the body through which *qi* and blood pass. However, they exist separately from blood vessels and veins. Meridians are divided into two types, called channels and collaterals. Channels are the longitudinal main lines, and collaterals are the branches of the channels, reaching to every part of the body. Besides circulating *qi* and blood, the meridians connect the viscera with the extremities and join up all the tissues, organs, tendons, skin and bones to form a whole organic unity.

One may liken the meridian system to a network of tributaries, or to use another useful image, to gutters or drains which link up to main canals. Their source comes internally from the five *zang* and six *fu* organs, and as a complete unit they work to reinforce the coordination and balance of the bodily functions.

The Functions of the Meridians

Other than the *qi* and blood which support the body's nutritional supply and other functions, there exists what is called *defensive qi* in the meridians, which circulates superficially. The *defensive qi* protects the body against exogenous pathogens. Through the network of meridians and channels, the whole body is under the protection of the circulating *defensive qi*.

Another important function of the meridians is to help doctors determine the source of a particular problem. Thus diseases of the affected *zang-fu* organs may be reflected on the body surface. Disorders of the five *zang* organs often show physical signs along the related meridians. For example, low back pain may occur in kidney disease, and chest pain may be noticed in heart and lung diseases. This is because the meridians, passing information of what is happening inside the body, will affect other parts of the body and therefore provide valuable information for diagnosis.

The theory of meridians is the framework for syndrome differentiation and diagnosis in every discipline of TCM, whether it be internal medicine, surgery, acupuncture or massage therapy. One cannot over-emphasize the close relation between the meridians and acupuncture. Once the meridian involved in disease is identified according to the meridian theory, appropriate treatment involving acupuncture, applied to the respective meridian, is the classical approach in TCM.

Regular Meridians and Extra-Meridians

There are twelve regular or main meridians in the human body. Regular meridians are directly related to the respective *zang-fu* organs after which they are named (e.g. *heart, lung, large intestine, small intestine*, etc.). Each specific *zang-fu* meridian is grouped into *yin* and *yang* according to their distribution. There are three pairs of *yin* and another three pairs of *yang* meridians. *Taiyin, Shaoyin* and *Jueyin* are the three *yins* while *Taiyang, Yangming* and *Shaoyang* are the three *yangs*. These meridians pass through the body and four limbs. Those traversing the upper limbs are called the three Hand meridians (Fig. 9.5); while those transversing the lower limbs are called the three Foot meridians (Fig. 9.7).

Apart from regular meridians, there are eight extra-meridians. Unlike the regular meridians, extra-meridians are not directly related to the internal organs. Interlacing with the twelve regular meridians, extra-meridians help each other to regulate their functions. A metaphoric comparison is that the 12 meridians are rivers, while the eight extra-meridians are lakes. The Conception Vessel or *Ren* Meridian (Fig. 9.9) and the Governor Vessel or *Du* Meridian (Fig. 9.8) from the eight extra-meridians together with the twelve meridians are grouped as the 14 most important meridians of the human body.

Recent Research on the Meridians

In recent years, much effort has been put into research on the meridians. Though some clues have already been found, it is still early to be able to unveil the mystery of meridians and collaterals. Much remains to be explored in this respect. The following gives an introduction to what has been achieved in the past three decades

Since 1958, propagation phenomena along the running course of the meridians have been reported in patients receiving acupuncture. Throbbing pain, red or white lines, dermatosis, alopecia have been noticed along the meridians in hundreds of reports in China. From 1958 to 1977, 3,000 out of 178,000 subjects or 1.7 per cent of the group investigated have been identified to have shown propagation phenomena along the meridians. Mechanical pressure was reported to be able to block or change the direction of the propagated sensation. Procaine might also block the propagation sensation in a great majority of the subjects during acupuncture. Average transmission speed of needling sensation is 20 centimetres per second, which is much slower than the transmission speed of trunk nerves (60 metres/sec) and that of internal viscera nerves (3–4 metres/sec). Thus neurotransmission cannot account for all propagation phenomena.

Three hundred and twenty-four frequently used acupuncture points have been dissected to discover their anatomical relationship with the nerves, blood vessels and lymphatics. Nerve roots of varying sizes were detected nearby in 323 cases. Dissection along the paths of the meridians also revealed major blood vessels or nerves underneath. The course of meridians occasionally was found to be similar to the route of the lymphatics, suggesting that the meridians are related to, though not identical with, nerves and blood vessels.

The electric resistance of the skin is lowest at the acupuncture points. While the resting electric potential is already higher at the acupoint than the neighbouring area, the potential difference exaggerates during acupuncture when the acupuncture sensation arrives (arrival of *qi*). A meridian may be looked upon as a special circuit for biological electric current, while the acupoints are the gates through which strong electric current flows. Electrocutaneous stimulation or acupuncture may alter the conductivity at acupuncture points and restore the usual electroactivity so as to achieve therapeutic effects.

All these phenomena provide observable evidences of the presence of the meridians. The exact nature of meridians and collaterals, however, remains a mystery pending further study and experimentation.

The Development of Acupuncture and Moxibustion

Based on archaeological studies of unearthed artifacts, the practice of acupuncture and moxibustion therapy has been dated back to very early in China. It is postulated that in the Stone Age, the ancient Chinese, through empirical experience, related recovery from disease and relief of pain to injuries at specific points in the body inflicted by stones or sharp edges. This is probably how the story of "puncture" or "acupuncture" began. The primitive acupuncture needles were made of stone and hence they were called stone needles. Thereafter with advances in metallurgy, metals replaced stone as the material for needles. In the TCM classic text, the *Nei Jing*, nine different types of needle designs were recorded. They were: the arrow-head needle, the round needle, the blunt needle, the sharp-edged needle, the sword-shaped needle, the round sharp needle, the filiform needle, the long needle and the large needle. Since then, the quality and design of the needles have become more and more sophisticated with the advances in technology. Gold, silver and stainless steel are now used to make the filiform needle, the three-edged needle, the subcutaneous needle and the intradermal needle. (See also page 192.)

The discovery of moxibustion therapy has also been attributed to the experiences of our ancestors when they found that relief from certain types of ailments could be facilitated by the scorching of their skin. The invention of moxibustion therefore probably started after practice of cooking was developed in China. Later moxa leaf was used for burning, which has the property of being able to release heat slowly and gently. This mild heat penetrates the skin and dispels the *cold* pathogens, thus activating the flow of *qi* and restoring the proper functioning of the meridians and collaterals. Moxa leaf was thereafter used as the raw material for moxibustion. Various herbs were then blended with moxa to enhance its therapeutic effects as the techniques of moxibustion advanced. The initial practice of moxibustion was direct scorching of the skin with burning moxa, which scarred the skin. Later, moxa was applied indirectly to the skin on top of a piece of raw ginger or garlic. An alternative way of moxibustion was removing the burning moxa as soon as the patient could no longer tolerate the heat. This non-scarring, non-blistering technique soon became widely acceptable to patients as a means of therapy. Moxibustion is more often indicated for chronic illnesses and diseases with *yang* deficiency. The treatment results of diseases such as chronic rheumatism, diarrhea and stomach diseases are good.

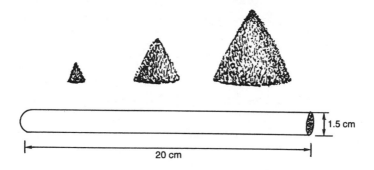

1.5 cm

20 cm

Fig. 9.1 Moxa cones & moxa stick

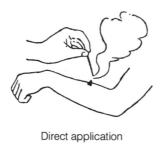

Direct application

Indirect, warming method

Fig. 9.2 The application of moxibustion

The Application of Acupuncture

The scope of indications of acupuncture is extensive. Recent advances in the understanding of acupuncture have widened its applications. In internal medicine, acupuncture is used to treat different kinds of pain, arthralgia, gastrointestinal diseases, asthma, apoplexy and enuresis. In surgery, acupuncture may be used to treat abdominal pain, uncomplicated appendicitis and cholecystitis. It is also used for gynecological diseases such as dysmenorrhea, amenorrhea and leukorrhea. In pediatrics, acupuncture is useful for controlling and treating convulsion, malnutrition and poliomyelitis. The therapeutic effects of acupuncture on acute infectious conjunctivitis, tonsillitis and toothache have also been good.

With the discovery of the analgesic effects of acupuncture, the procedure has been used extensively in surgical operations since 1958. Reassuring results have been documented in both minor and major operations, such as tonsillectomy, thyroidectomy, gastrectomy, pneumonectomy and neurosurgery. In contrast to general anesthesia, the patient receiving acupuncture analgesia remains conscious and may cooperate with the surgeon throughout the operation. There have been few post-operative complications and the recovery rate of the patients has been fast. The success of acupuncture as an analgesia has created extensive interest in this field both in China and overseas.

Starting in the 1960's, research has been carried out regarding the study of how acupuncture actually works as an analgesia. Preliminary research showed that body fluids contain analgesic ingredients which are induced by acupuncture. Research into the mechanism by which acupuncture works is still continuing. An increasing number of neurochemical transmitters have been identified and evaluated for their actions and interactions with other neurotransmitters. Readers are encouraged to refer to recent literature in professional journals on pain research and acupuncture. An excellent review of the topic is Lu Gwei-Djen and Joseph Needham's book, *Celestial Lancets — A History and Rationale of Acupuncture and Moxa.*

Acupoints

Acupoints are specific spots where the *qi* of the *zang-fu* organs, channels and collaterals accumulates, and are therefore the sites where acupuncture is applied. Acupoints or *shu* in Chinese literally means "transport" while point or *xue* means "fissure". Acupoints are also called *qi* points, hole points and bone clefts but are more commonly called acupuncture points.

Function of Acupoints

Acupoints are located all along the channels and collaterals. Hence their functions are closely related to those of the meridian system. As stated earlier channels and collaterals are the routes along which *qi* and *blood* circulate. The acupoints can be looked upon as stations via which the *qi* and *blood* in the channel system are transported. When a *zang-fu* organ is sick, there are abnormal changes in certain acupoints along the corresponding channel, such as a tenderness or hypersensitivity to stimulation. Acupuncture achieves its effect by means of stimulating these spots in order to regulate the functioning of the channels and *zang-fu* organs.

Every acupoint can be used to treat local diseases involving the areas around the point. Thus the points in the chest are often used to treat thoracic (including internal organs) diseases. The points in the abdomen generally apply to treating abdominal and visceral diseases. Those on the face, head and ear may be used to treat diseases of the face, head and ear respectively.

The acupuncture points of the four limbs, especially those below the elbow and the knee, yield not only local but also distant therapeutic effects on the head, face and the trunk. These special effects are closely related to the channel and collateral system. For instance, the points of the four limbs of the Hand Three *Yin* meridians can serve to treat chest diseases according to the routing of the channel, while the points of the four limbs of the Hand Three *Yang* meridians are useful for head diseases.

Various Kinds of Acupoints

There are three different kinds of acupoints:

1.   *Channel points*: These pertain to the points along the fourteen channels. There are 361 points in all.

2.   *Extraordinary points*: These are the points that do not belong to the system of the fourteen meridians. The total number is about 200.

3.   *Ashi points*: They are the points without definite anatomical positions. Their locations are defined by where there is tenderness and reaction on palpation or stimulation. The *ashi* points are also referred to as tender points or *tian yin* points.

Locating the Acupoints

There are hundreds of acupuncture points on the human body, therefore accurately locating the points directly affects the therapeutic effects. In order to cite the points correctly, one must master the measurement criteria of acupuncture points. There are a number of mapping standards. The most widely used method is referring to the patient's own finger as the standard length of measurement. The unit measurement in acupuncture is called *cun* (approximately equal to one-third of a decimetre) and there are two different versions of its definition:

1. *Middle Finger Measurement*: A *cun* is the distance between the medial flexures of the proximal and distal interphalangeal joints of the middle finger of the patient. The *cun* thus defined may be used to locate the vertical distances of the acupoints in the limbs as well as the horizontal distances of the acupoints at the back.

2. *Four-finger Measurement*: This is also called the "finger breadth measurement". The breadth of the four fingers of the patient's hand, held closely together at the level of the proximal interphalangeal joints is defined as three *cuns*.

one cun

One *cun* (or Chinese inch) according to the middle finger measurement of a patient for locating the acupoints

Fig. 9.3 Middle finger measurement

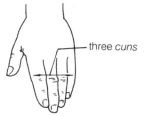
three *cuns*

Three *cuns* according to the breadth of the four fingers of a patient for locating the acupoints

Fig. 9.4 Four-finger measurement

Acupuncture points may also be located through surface anatomy. For instance, the *Tanzhong* acupoint (CV 17) (Fig.9.9) is midway in between the two nipples. The *Baihui* acupoint (Gv 20) (Fig. 9.6) is at the vertex of the skull above the apexes of the two ears. *Houxi* (SI 3) (Fig. 9.5) is at the tip of the transverse palmer crease of the fist.

Routes of the Fourteen Channels and the Acupoints

The Lung Channel of the Hand Taiyin or the Lung Meridian

This originates from the abdomen, passes through the axilla and descends along the anteromedial aspect of the upper arm, elbow and the forearm to the lateral side of the nail of the thumb. There are 11 acupoints along the Lung meridian. The most commonly used points are the following, with their specific indications.

1. *Chize* (L 5): This is located lateral to the biceps along the elbow crease of the cubital fossa. (Fig. 9.5)
    Indications: Coughs, asthma, fullness and distension in the chest and hypochondrium, spasm and pain in the elbow and arm, apoplexy and hemiplegia.
    Acupuncture: Depth of puncture is 0.3–0.5 inch.

2. *Lieque* (L 7): 1.5 *cuns* above the transverse crease of the wrist. This is where the index finger is tipping when the index finger and the thumb of one hand cross with those of the other. (Fig. 9.5)
    Indications: Headache, migraine, cough, hemiplegia, deviation of the eyes and mouth, elbow pain and dysuria.

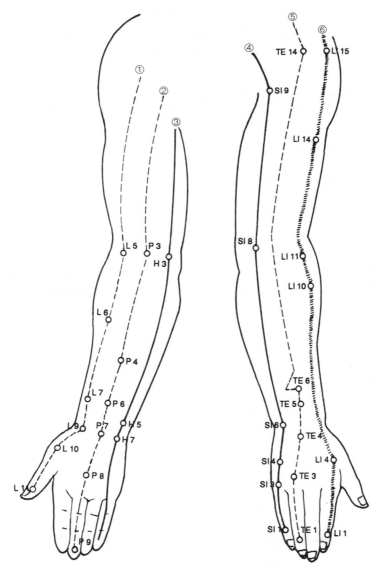

Fig. 9.5 Distribution of acupoints along six of the fourteen meridians on the upper limbs

1   (L) The Lung Meridian of Hand *Taiyin*
2   (P) The Pericardium Meridian of Hand *Juejin*
3   (H) The Heart Meridian of Hand *Shaoyin*
4   (SI) The Small Intestine Meridian of Hand *Taiyang*
5   (TE) The Triple Energizer or *Sanjiao* Meridian of Hand *Shaoyang*
6   (LI) The Large Intestine Meridian of Hand *Yangming*

Acupuncture and Moxibustion: Puncture 0.2–0.3 inch with the needle pointing obliquely upward to the elbow. Duration of moxibustion is 3 to 7 moxa cones.

3. *Shaoshang* (L 11): The location is on the radial aspect of the thumb, about 0.1 *cun* posterior to the corner of the nail. (Fig. 9.5)
    Indications: apoplexy, coma, epistaxis, sore throat and fever.
    Acupuncture: Puncture 0.1 inch with the needle directing slightly upwards.

The Large Intestine Meridian of the Hand Yangming

This starts from the tip of the index finger and proceeds upward along the radial side of the index finger, passing in between the first and second metacarpals, and then along the anterolateral side of the forearm to the lateral side of the elbow. From there, it climbs along the lateral anterior aspect of the upper arm to the *Dazhui* acupoint (Gv 14) (Fig. 9.8) through the acromion at the highest point of the shoulder. After descending to the supraclavicular fossa, it divides into two branches. One slides through the chest to the large intestine and the other one ascends to the neck. There are 20 points in this meridian. Among these points, the most commonly used are:

1. *Hegu* (LI 4): This is located in between the first and second metacarpals at the depression exposed when the index finger and the thumb open slightly.(Fig. 9.5)
    Indications: Headache, nebula, epistaxis, deafness, toothache, slight sweating in *heat* syndromes, amenorrhea and apoplexy.
    Acupuncture and Moxibustion: Depth of puncture is 0.3–0.7 inch. Moxibustion time is 3 to 7 moxa cones. This point is contraindicated in pregnancy.

2. *Quchi* (LI 11): With the elbow flexed, *Quchi* is at the lateral end of the transverse fold of the elbow. (Fig. 9.5) Indications: Swelling and pain of the hand and arm, hemiparesis and urticaria.
Acupuncture and Moxibustion: Depth of puncture is 0.8–1.5 inches. Moxibustion time is 3 to 7 moxa cones.

3. *Jianyu* (LI 15): The point is located anterior to the acromion of the shoulder at the depression which appears when the arm is set horizontally. (Fig. 9.5) Indications: Pain in the shoulder and arm, hemiparesis and urticaria.
Acupuncture and moxibustion: Depth of puncture is 0.6–1.5 inches. Moxibustion time is 7 to 17 moxa cones.

The Stomach Meridian of the Foot Yangming

This meridian ascends from the lateral side of the nose to the nasal root. Descending along the lateral side of the nose, another branch enters the upper gum and then circles back around the corner of the mouth. From here, it follows the angle of the jaw and runs upward in front of the ear. It proceeds along the hairline and crosses to the middle of the forehead, parallel with the frontal hairline.

One branch descends along the throat, enters the supraclavicular fossa, passes through the diaphragm and finally enters the stomach.

Another vertical branch descends directly from the supraclavicular fossa along the mammillary line, then passes beside the umbilicus and through the lower abdomen to the inguinal region.

A final branch begins at the pylorus and descends in the abdomen to the inguinal region. It then descends again directly to the patella along the anterior aspect of the thigh and then along the lateral side of the tibia to the dorsum of the foot, ending at the lateral side of the tip of the second

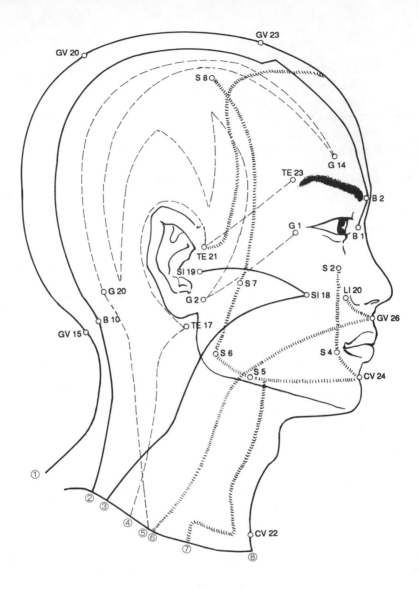

Fig. 9.6 Distribution of acupoints along eight of the fourteen meridians on the head, face, neck and nape

1   (GV) The Governor Vessel or *Du* Meridian
2   (B) The Bladder Meridian of Foot *Taiyang*
3   (SI) The Small Intestine Meridian of Hand *Taiyang*
4   (TE) The Triple Energizer or *Sanjiao* Meridian of Hand *Shaoyang*
5   (G) The Gallbladder Meridian of Foot *Shaoyang*
6   (LI) The Large Intestine Meridian of Hand *Yangming*
7   (S) The Stomach Meridian of Foot *Yangming*
8   (CV) The Conception Vessel or *Ren* Meridian

toe. There are 45 points along the channel. The most commonly used are:

1. *Dicang* (S 4): This is 0.4 *cun* lateral to the corner of the mouth. (Fig. 9.6)
   Indications: Bell's palsy and salivation.
   Acupuncture and Moxibustion: Puncture 0.3-0.7 inch with the needle tip directing obliquely towards the *Jianche* point (S 6). The duration of moxibustion is 3 to 7 moxa cones.

2. *Jianche* (S 6): This is 0.5 *cun* anterior to the lower angle of the mandible, at the prominence of the masseter muscle when teeth are clenched. (Fig. 9.6)
   Indications: Bell's palsy, trismus, toothache and swollen cheeks.
   Acupuncture and Moxibustion: Puncture 0.4 inch with the needle tip directing obliquely towards the *Dicang* point (S 4). The length of moxibustion is 3 to 7 moxa cones.

3. *Tianshu* (S 25): This position is 2 *cuns* lateral to the centre of the umbilicus. (Fig. 9.9)
   Indications: Vomiting, diarrhea, borborygmus, abdominal distension and pain around the umbilicus.
   Acupuncture and Moxibustion: Puncture depth is 0.5– 1.0 inch. Apply moxibustion with 7 to 15 moxa cones.

4. *Zusanli* (S 36): This is 3 *cuns* below the *Dubi* (S 35) point. It is a general tonifying point. (Fig. 9.7)
   Indications: Epigastric pain, abdominal pain, indigestion, borborygmus, diarrhea, apoplexy and hemiplegia.
   Acupuncture and Moxibustion: Puncture depth is 0.5– 1.0 inch. Apply moxibustion with 7 to 20 moxa cones.

5. *Fenglong* (S 40): This is 8 *cuns* above the external malleolus. (Fig. 9.7)

Indications: Asthma, shortness of breath, profuse sputum, vomiting, constipation, mania and epilepsy.
Acupuncture and Moxibustion: Puncture depth is 0.5–1.0 inch. Length of moxibustion is 7 to 15 moxa cones.

6. *Neiting* (S 44): This point is at the proximal end of the second web space between the second and the third toes. (Fig.9.7)
    Indications: Pain at the dorsum of the foot, toothache, epigastric pain, diarrhea and dysentery.
    Acupuncture and Moxibustion: Puncture depth is 0.3–0.5 inch. Apply moxibustion with 3 to 5 moxa cones.

The Spleen Meridian of the Foot Taiyin

Beginning from the medial tip of the big toe, this meridian runs upwards along the first metatarsal bone. It passes in front of the medial malleolus and ascends along the posterior side of the tibia and the anteromedial aspect of the thigh. Through the abdomen, it arrives at the chest where a tributary ascends to the root of the tongue. A branch of the meridian separates in the stomach region and finds its way both to the spleen as well as the heart after crossing the diaphragm. There are 21 points along the channel. The commonly used points are as follows:

1. *Yinbai* (Sp 1): This point is situated at the medial part of the big toe, about 0.1 *cun* lateral to the lower corner of the nail. (Fig. 9.7)
    Indications: Diarrhea, menorrhagia, seizure and mania.
    Acupuncture and Moxibustion: The depth of puncture is 0.1–0.2 inch. Apply moxibustion with 2 to 3 moxa cones.

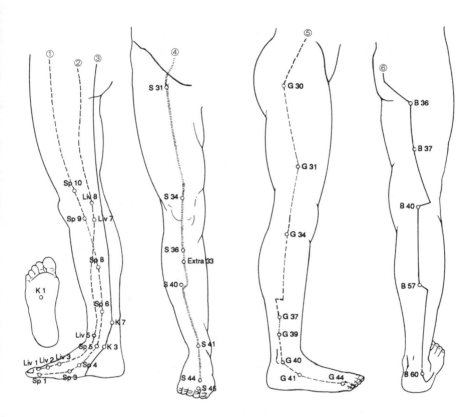

Fig. 9.7 Distribution of acupoints along six of the fourteen meridians on the lower limbs

1 (Sp) The Spleen Meridian of Foot *Taiyin*
2 (Liv) The Liver Meridian of Foot *Jueyin*
3 (K) The Kidney Meridian of Foot *Shaoyin*
4 (S) The Stomach Meridian of Foot *Yangming*
5 (G) The Gallbladder Meridian of Foot *Shaoyang*
6 (B) The Bladder Meridian of Foot *Taiyang*

2. *Gongsun* (Sp 4): This is one *cun* anterior to the first metatarsal head.
    Indications: Epigastric and abdominal pain. (Fig. 9.7)
    Acupuncture and Moxibustion: The depth of puncture is 0.5 inch. Apply moxibustion with 3 to 5 moxa cones.

3. *Sanyinjiao* (Sp 6): The location is 3 *cuns* directly above the tip of the medial malleolus. (Fig. 9.7)
    Indications: Menorrhagia, seminal emission, premature ejaculation, enuresis, indigestion and epigastric pain.
    Acupuncture and Moxibustion: The depth of puncture is 0.5–0.8 inch. Apply moxibustion with 5 to 10 moxa cones. This point should not be used for patients who are pregnant.

4. *Yinlingquan* (Sp 9): With the leg stretched out, the point is in the depression on the medial border of the tibia. (Fig. 9.7)
    Indications: Seminal emission, enuresis, edema, back and leg pain.
    Acupuncture: The depth of puncture is 0.5 inch.

The Heart Meridian of the Hand Shaoyin

Starting from the heart, the Heart meridian passes through the great blood vessel system of the heart and diaphragm to the small intestine. A branch comes directly from the heart, and then slants downward to emerge below the axilla. There it descends along the posteromedial aspect of the upper arm and palm to the lateral side of the little finger and to the fingertip. There are 9 points all together. The commonly used points are as follows:

1. *Shaohai* (H 3): With the elbow flexed, this point is located at the medial end of the transverse cubital crease. (Fig. 9.5)

Indications: Pain in the chest, vomiting and numbness of the arm.

Acupuncture and Moxibustion: The depth of puncture is 0.5–0.8 inch. Apply moxibustion with 3 to 5 moxa cones.

2. *Tongli* (H 5): The point is 1 *cun* proximal to the ulnar end of the wrist crease. (Fig. 9.5)

    Indications: Palpitation, aphonia, pain in the medial side of the elbow and arm.

    Acupuncture and Moxibustion: Puncture 0.3 inch deep. Apply moxibustion with 3 moxa cones.

3. *Shenmen* (H 7): This is situated proximal to the pisiform bone in the wrist. (Fig. 9.5)

    Indications: Palpitation, anxiety, angina pectoris, amnesia and insomnia.

    Acupuncture and Moxibustion: The puncture depth is 0.3 inch. Length of moxibustion is 3 moxa cones.

The Small Intestine Meridian of the Hand Taiyang

This meridian originates at the ulnar side of the tip of the little finger. Ascending along the ulnar side of the hand to the wrist, it climbs up along the posterior medial side of the forearm. Through the elbow, the meridian ascends along the posterior lateral aspect of the upper arm to the shoulder. It continues its route through the scapula to the supraclavicular fossa where it penetrates into the body and descends along the esophagus to the small intestine. Among the 19 points along the channel, the most commonly used points are as follows:

1. *Houxi* (SI 3): This point is at the depression at the lateral side proximal to the fifth metacarpophalangeal joint. (Fig. 9.5)

Indications: Spasms of the fingers, fever and night sweats.

Acupuncture and Moxibustion: The depth of puncture is 0.5–0.8 inch. The length of moxibustion is 3 to 7 moxa cones.

2.   *Yanglao* (SI 6): With the palm facing the chest, the point is in the bony seam on the radial side of the styloid process of the ulna. (Fig. 9.5)

Indications: Blurring of vision, chronic eye diseases, pain in the shoulder and arm.

Acupuncture and Moxibustion: The depth of puncture is 0.1–0.2 inch. Apply moxibustion with 3 moxa cones.

3.   *Jianzhen* (SI 9): This point is underneath the shoulder joint. With arm hanging freely at the side, the point is 1 *cun* above the posterior end of the axillary fold. (Fig. 9.5)

Indications: Tinnitus, deafness and pain in the scapula.

Acupuncture: The depth of puncture is 0.5 to 1.0 inch.

The Bladder Meridian of the Foot Taiyang

This meridian starts at the inner canthus of the eye, and ascends across the forehead and reaches the vertex. The two vertical branches descend through the back of the neck to the trunk parallel to the spine and to the gluteal region and join together at the popliteal fossa. The meridian continues its route behind the leg. Emerging behind the lateral malleolus of the fibula, the meridian travels on the lateral side of the foot and ends at the lateral tip of the little toe. There are all together 67 points on the channel. The most commonly used are:

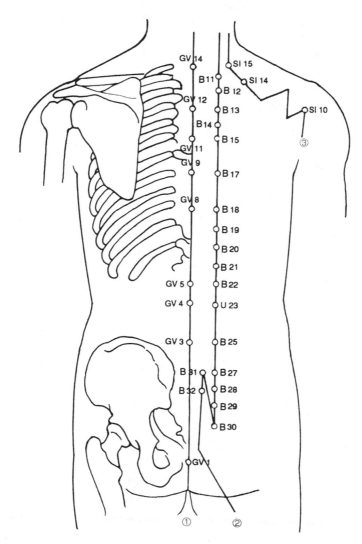

Fig. 9.8 Distribution of acupoints along three of the fourteen meridians on the shoulder, back, waist and sacrum

1. (GV) The Governor Vessel or *Du* Meridian
2. (B) The Bladder Meridian of Foot *Taiyang*
3. (SI) The Small Intestine Meridian of Hand *Taiyang*

1. *Feishu* (B 13): This point is 1.5 *cuns* lateral to the lower end of the spinal process of the third thoracic vertebra. (Fig. 9.8)
    Indications: Cough, hemoptysis, shortness of breath, tuberculosis and night sweats.
    Acupuncture and moxibustion: The depth of puncture is 0.5 inch. Apply moxibustion with 5 to 15 moxa cones.

2. *Xinshu* (B 15): This is situated 1.5 *cuns* lateral to the lower end of the spinal process of the fifth thoracic vertebra. (Fig. 9.8)
    Indications: Cough, hemoptysis, mental confusion, amnesia and epilepsy.
    Acupuncture and Moxibustion: The depth of puncture is 0.3 inch. Apply moxibustion with 3 to 7 moxa cones.

3. *Ganshu* (B 18): This is 1.5 *cuns* lateral to the lower end of the spinal process of the ninth thoracic vertebra. (Fig. 9.8)
    Indications: Jaundice, blurring of vision, red swollen eyes, and mania.
    Acupuncture and Moxibustion: The depth of puncture is 0.5 inch. Apply moxibustion with 3 to 7 moxa cones.

4. *Danshu* (B 19): The location of this point is 1.5 *cuns* lateral to the lower end of the spinal process of the tenth thoracic vertebra. (Fig. 9.8)
    Indications: Jaundice, chest and hypochondriac pain, bitter taste in the mouth, loss of appetite and vomiting.
    Acupuncture and Moxibustion: The depth of puncture is 0.5 inch. Apply moxibustion with 3 to 7 moxa cones.

5. *Pishu* (B 20): This point is located 1.5 *cuns* lateral to the lower end of the spinal process of the eleventh thoracic vertebra. (Fig. 9.8)
    Indications: Indigestion, abdominal distension, diarrhea, hiccups and edema.

Acupuncture and Moxibustion: The depth of puncture is 0.5 inch. Apply moxibustion with 3 to 7 moxa cones.

6. *Weishu* (B 21): The location of this point is 1.5 *cuns* lateral to the lower end of the spinal process of the twelfth thoracic vertebra. (Fig. 9.8)
    Indications: Regurgitation, vomiting, stomach *cold* and loss of appetite.
    Acupuncture and Moxibustion: The depth of puncture is 0.5 inch. Apply moxibustion with 3 to 7 moxa cones.

7. *Shenshu* (B 23): This is 1.5 *cuns* lateral to the lower end of the spinal process of the second lumbar vertebra. (Fig. 9.8)
    Indications: Seminal emission, impotence, hematuria, back pain due to kidney deficiency, deafness, blurring of vision and edema.
    Acupuncture and Moxibustion: The depth of puncture is 0.5 inch. Apply moxibustion with 3 to 7 moxa cones.

8. *Dachangshu* (B 25): The location of this point is 1.5 *cuns* lateral to the lower end of the spinal process of the fourth lumbar vertebra. (Fig. 9.8)
    Indications: Borborygmus, abdominal distension, peri-umbilical pain, diarrhea, constipation and low back pain.
    Acupuncture and Moxibustion: The depth of puncture is 0.5 inch. Apply moxibustion with 5 to 15 moxa cones.

9. *Weizhong* (B 40): This point is at the midpoint of the transverse crease of the popliteal fossa. (Fig. 9.7)
    Indications: Low back pain, motor impairment of the knee joint, hemiplegia, acute vomiting and diarrhea, chest pain and abdominal colic, febrile diseases without sweating.
    Acupuncture and Moxibustion: Puncture 1.0–1.5 inches deep. Moxibustion is contraindicated.

The Kidney Meridian of the Foot Shaoyin

This kidney meridian starts underneath the little toe. Crossing obliquely the plantar surface of the foot to the depression in front of the navicular bone, it emerges behind the medial malleous to the medial surface of the lower limb and ascends to the medial side of the knee. The channel divides into two. One branch penetrates into the abdomen and ends in the kidney while the other branch continues its ascending route from the abdomen to the chest. There are 27 points on the channel. The more commonly used points are:

1. *Yongquan* (K 1): This point lies in the depression in the plantar surface when the foot is flexed. (Fig. 9.7)
    Indications: Headache at the vertex, blurring of vision and seizure in infants. Moxibustion may be performed before going to bed.
    Acupuncture and Moxibustion: The depth of puncture is 0.3–0.5 inch. Apply moxibustion with 3 to 7 moxa cones.

2. *Taixi* (K 3): The location of *Taixi* is 0.5 *cun* posterior to the medial malleolus. (Fig. 9.7)
    Indications: Pharyngitis, cough, hematemesis, kidney deficiency, impotence, irregular menstruation and somnolence.
    Acupuncture and Moxibustion: The depth of puncture is 0.5 inch. The needle tip is directed to the anterior border of the lateral malleolus. Apply moxibustion with 7 to 15 moxa cones.

3. *Fuliu* (K 7): This point is directly above the *Taixi* (K 3), 2 *cuns* above the level of the medial malleolus. (Fig. 9.7)
    Indications: Edema, night sweats and low back pain.
    Acupuncture and Moxibustion: The depth of puncture

is 0.3–0.5 inch. Apply moxibustion with 7 to 15 moxa cones.

The Pericardium Meridian of the Hand Jueyin

This meridian begins in the chest where it joins with the pericardium collateral. One branch descends to the diaphragm and joins with the *sanjiao* in the abdomen. The main branch runs along the chest and emerges from the costal region at a point 3 *cuns* below the anterior axillary fold before ascending to the inferior aspect of the axilla. From there, it descends along the medial aspect of the upper arm to the antecubital fossa, and then proceeds down the forearm between the palmaris longus and flexor carpi radialis muscles. Entering the palm, it follows the ulnar aspect of the middle finger until it reaches the fingertip. There are 9 points along this meridian. The most frequently used are as follows:

1. *Quze* (P 3): With the elbow flexed, the point is at the centre of the transverse crease of the elbow, on the medial side of the tendon of the biceps muscle. (Fig. 9.5)
   Indications: Angina pectoris and palpitation.
   Acupuncture and Moxibustion: The depth of puncture is 0.3–0.5 inch. Apply moxibustion with 3 to 7 moxa cones.

2. *Neiguan* (P 6): The point is 2 *cuns* proximal to the midpoint of the transverse crease of the wrist between the palmaris longus and flexor carpi radialis. (Fig. 9.5)
   Indications: Angina pectoris, anxiety, epilepsy, regurgitation, vomiting and pain in the chest and costal region.
   Acupuncture and Moxibustion: The depth of puncture is 0.5 inch. Apply moxibustion with 3 to 7 moxa cones.

3.   *Laogong* (P 8): With the middle finger and the ring finger fully flexed, the point is between the tips of the two fingers. (Fig. 9.5)

Indications: Angina pectoris, anxiety, palpitation, hand tremors and tinea unguium.

Acupuncture and Moxibustion: The depth of puncture is 0.3–0.5 inch. Apply moxibustion with 3 to 7 moxa cones.

The Triple Energizer (Sanjiao) Meridian of the Hand Shaoyang

This starts from the ulnar side of the ring finger tip and ascends along the dorsum of the wrist and the forearm between the radius and ulna to the olecranon process. Reaching the shoulder after climbing its way along the lateral side of the arm, it changes course to the supraclavicular fossa. One branch winds behind the ear to end up at the infraorbital area. Winding over to the supraclavicular fossa, it then descends through the diaphragm to the abdomen linking successively with the upper, middle and lower *jiao*. A branch emerges from the supraclavicular fossa and then ascends to the neck, running along the posterior border of the ear, and further to the corner of the anterior hairline. Then it turns downward to the cheek and ends in the infraorbital region. There are all together 23 points. The most frequently used are:

1.   *Waiguan* (TE 5): This point is 2 *cuns* proximal to the centre of the dorsal transverse crease of the wrist between the ulna and radius. (Fig. 9.5)

Indications: Headache, tinnitus, deafness, motor impairment of the elbow and arm, pain of the finger and hand tremors.

Acupuncture and Moxibustion: The depth of puncture is 0.5–0.8 inch. Apply moxibustion with 3 to 7 moxa cones.

2.   *Zhigou* (TE 6): Located between the ulna and radius, the point is 1 *cun* proximal to the *Waiguan* (TE 5) point. (Fig. 9.5)

Indications: Pain in the hypochondriac regions, chest pain, vomiting, soreness and pain in the shoulder and arm.

Acupuncture and Moxibustion: The depth of puncture is 0.5–0.8 inch. Apply moxibustion with 3 to 7 moxa cones.

3.   *Yifeng* (TE 17): This point is located in the depression anterior to the mastoid process and posterior to the earlobe when the mouth is open. (Fig. 9.6)

Indications: Tinnitus, deafness and deviation of the eye and mouth.

Acupuncture and Moxibustion: The point should be punctured with the mouth open and the depth of puncture is 0.3–0.5 inch. Apply moxibustion with 3 to 5 moxa cones.

4.   *Sizhukong* (TE 23): This point is located at the depression of the lateral end of the eyebrow. (Fig. 9.6)

Indications: Migraine, headache and eye pain.

Acupuncture and Moxibustion: The depth of puncture is 0.3–0.5 inch in the subcutaneous plane.

The Gallbladder Meridian of the Foot Shaoyang

Starting from the outer canthus of the eye, the Gallbladder meridian ascends to the corner of the forehead and then descends posterior to the ear and along the lateral side of the neck to the shoulder. It then turns anterior and enters the supraclavicular fossa, which pertains to the gallbladder. A branch runs downward from the supraclavicular fossa to the axilla and lateral aspect of the chest. It zigzags its way to the hip and descends along the lateral side of the lower limb. The meridian places itself anterior to the fibula and reaches the foot anterior to the lateral malleolus of the fibula. It crosses the dorsum of the foot and terminates at the lateral side of the tip of the fourth toe. There are 44 points along the Gallbladder meridian. The most frequently used are as follows:

1. *Fengchi* (G 20): This point is in the depression between the lateral aspect of the trapezius muscle and the mastoid process of the skull. (Fig. 9.6)
    Indications: Headache, stiff neck, red and painful eyes, apoplexy, febrile disease without sweating.
    Acupuncture and Moxibustion: The point should be accessed obliquely at a depth of 0.5–0.8 inch. Apply moxibustion with 3 to 7 moxa cones.

2. *Huantiao* (G 30): The patient is positioned in the lateral decubitus position with the upper leg flexed at the hip and knee. The point lies on the lateral third of the line joining the greater trochanter and the caudal end of the sacrum. (Fig. 9.7)
    Indications: Lumbosacral pain, leg pain and hemiplegia.
    Acupuncture and Moxibustion: The depth of puncture is 1.5–2.5 inches. Apply moxibustion with 10 to 20 moxa cones.

3. *Yanglingquan* (G 34): This point lies on the lateral side of the knee in the depression slightly anterior and inferior to the fibular head. (Fig. 9.7)
    Indications: Pain in the hypochondriac region, bitter taste in the mouth, hemiplegia and agonizing knee pain.
    Acupuncture and Moxibustion: The depth of puncture is 0.8–1.0 inch. Apply moxibustion with 5 to 7 moxa cones.

4. *Guangming* (G 37): This point is 5 *cuns* above the lateral malleolus of the fibula. (Fig. 9.7)
    Indications: Eye diseases and knee pain.
    Acupuncture: The depth of puncture is 0.5–0.6 inch. Apply moxibustion with 3 to 5 cones.

5. *Zulinqi* (G 41): Located at the depression between the distal heads of the fourth and fifth metatarsal bones. (Fig. 9.7)
    Indications: Blurring of vision and pain in the hypochondriac region.
    Acupuncture and Moxibustion: The depth of puncture is 0.3–0.5 inch. Apply moxibustion with 3 to 5 moxa cones.

The Liver Meridian of the Foot Jueyin

This starts from the hairy dorsal region of the big toe, ascends along the dorsum of the foot and in front of the medial malleolus to the medial side of the knee along the medial side of the tibia. The meridian climbs further upward to the pubic hair region. Winding around the genitalia, it enters the lower abdomen, where it meets the Stomach meridian and joins with the liver. A branch separates from the lower abdomen and ascends to the costal region. There are 14 points in all. The most commonly used points are as follows:

1. *Xingjian* (Liv 2): This point lies in the web between the first and the second toes. (Fig. 9.7)
    Indications: Red and painful eyes, pain in the hypochondriac region, insomnia and epilepsy.
    Acupuncture and Moxibustion: The depth of puncture is 0.3–0.4 inch. Apply moxibustion with 3 to 5 moxa cones.

2. *Taichong* (Liv 3): This point lies in between the anterior junction of the first and second metatarsal heads. (Fig. 9.7)

    Indications: Pain in the pubic area, enuresis, seizures in children.

    Acupuncture and Moxibustion: The depth of puncture is 0.3–0.4 inches. Apply moxibustion with 3 to 5 cones.

The Governor Vessel (Du) Meridian

Starting from a point in the perineum, the Governor Vessel or *Du* meridian emerges from the sacrococcyx and climbs upwards along the dorsal spine until it penetrates into the brain and reaches the vertex where it joins the other collaterals. Then it descends along the midline of the forehead and ends at the columnella of the nose. There are all together 28 points. The most frequently used are:

1. *Yaoyangguan* (GV 3): This is located below the spinal process of the fourth lumbar vertebra. (Fig. 9.8)

    Indications: Lumbago, menstrual disorders and leucorrhea.

    Acupuncture and Moxibustion: The depth of puncture is 0.5 inch. Apply moxibustion with 3 to 15 moxa cones.

2. *Mingmen* (GV 4): This point is below the spinal process of the second lumbar vertebra. (Fig. 9.8)

    Indications: Headache, opisthotonus, lumbago, seminal emission, and impotence.

    Acupuncture and Moxibustion: Puncture to a depth of 0.5–0.8 inch. Apply moxibustion with 3 to 15 moxa cones.

3. *Baihua* (GV 20): This point is situated at the intersection of the median line at the vertex of the head with a line drawn from the tip of one ear to the other. (Fig. 9.6)

Indications: Headache, blurring of vision, amnesia, apoplexy and rectal prolapse.

Acupuncture and Moxibustion: The point should be reached in the subcutaneous plane 0.3 inch under the skin. Apply moxibustion with 5 to 7 moxa cones.

4. *Renzhong* (GV 26): This point lies in the philtrum about one-third of the distance from the bottom of the nose to the top of the lip. (Fig. 9.6)

   Indications: Unconsciousness or coma due to various causes, mania, seizures in children, apoplexy and lockjaw.

   Acupuncture and Moxibustion: The depth of puncture is 0.2–0.3 inch. The needle should be punctured obliquely and upward until strong pain is felt.

The Conception Vessel (Ren) Meridian

This meridian arises from the perineum and runs forward to the hairy margin above the external genitalia. The meridian then ascends along the midline of the abdomen, crosses the throat, winds around the lips, passes through the cheek and finally enters the infraorbital region. There are 24 points along the meridian. The most frequently used points are:

1. *Guanyuan* (CV 4): This point is 3 *cuns* below the umbilicus. (Fig. 9.9)

   Indications: Menstrual disorder, morbid leucorrhea, seminal emission, lower abdominal pain, flaccid type of apoplexy, prolapse of rectum and all kinds of *deficiency* syndromes.

   Acupuncture and moxibustion: The depth of puncture is 0.8–1.0 inch. Apply moxibustion with 7 to 10 moxa cones.

2. *Zhongwan* (CV 12): This point is located 4 *cuns* above the umbilicus. (Fig. 9.9)
    Indications: Epigastric pain, abdominal distension, vomiting and indigestion.
    Acupuncture and Moxibustion: The depth of puncture is 1 inch. Apply moxibustion with 7 to 15 moxa cones.

3. *Tanzhong* (CV 17): This is found at the midpoint of the sternum at the level of the nipples. (Fig. 9.9)
    Indications: Asthma, insufficient lactation and chest pain.
    Acupuncture and Moxibustion: The depth of puncture is 0.3–0.5 inch. The needle should be inserted subcutaneously with the tip directed caudally. Apply moxibustion with 3 to 7 moxa cones.

Conclusion

Using the above-mentioned information, it has been determined that the distribution of the fourteen meridians conforms to the following rules:

1. The three hand *yin* meridians run from the chest and end at the fingers, while the three hand *yang* meridians run from the fingers and end at the head. The three foot *yang* meridians run from the head and end at the toe, while the three foot *yin* meridians run from the toe and end at the chest and abdomen.

2. The *yang* meridians travel along the lateral and dorsal surfaces of the body while the *yin* meridians essentially run on the medial and ventral surfaces.

3. *Taiyang* meridians run dorsally. *Yangming* meridians run ventrally while the *Shaoyang* meridians run laterally.

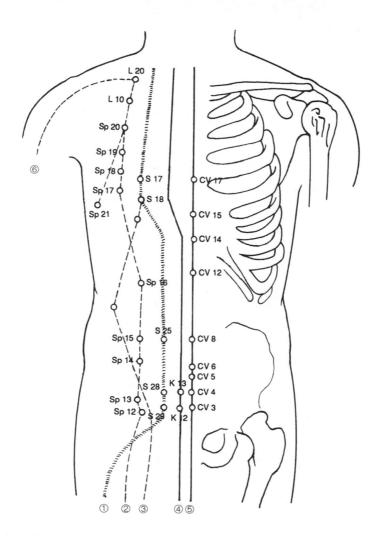

Fig. 9.9 Distribution of acupoints along six of the fourteen meridians on the chest, breast, rib and abdomen

1 (S) The Stomach Meridian of Foot *Yangming*
2 (Sp) The Spleen Meridian of Foot *Taiyin*
3 (Liv) The Liver Meridian of Foot *Jueyin*
4 (K) The Kidney Meridian of Foot *Shaoyin*
5 (CV) The Conception Vessel or *Ren* Meridian
6 (L) The Lung Meridian of Hand *Taiyin*

4. The Governor Vessel meridian runs along the midline of the back (Fig. 9.8), while the Conception Vessel meridian runs along the midline of the abdomen (Fig. 9.9).

Needling

In case of diseases, laying a needle onto the selected acupoints promotes free flow of *qi* and *blood* along the channels and collaterals. It also reinforces the harmony of both *qi* and *blood* in the body. This method of eliminating pathogenic factors for disease treatment is known as needling in the practice of acupuncture.

Commonly Used Acupuncture Needles Today

There are at least three classical types of acupuncture needles:

1. *The filiform needle*: The length of the filiform needle varies from 0.5 to 5 inches and the gauge ranges from Nos. 26 to 32. It has a round and smooth body. The material may be different metals. However the most common material used is stainless steel. The filiform needle is the most popular acupuncture needle used at present.

2. *The three-edged needle*: It has a body with a triangular cutting edge. The needle has different lengths and gauges. This type of needle is often used for blood letting by superficial pricking of the point in the treatment of *excess-heat* diseases.

3. *The cutaneous needle*: It is also called the infantile

needle. Five to seven micro needles bundled together at one end of a rod in the shape of the seedpod of the lotus, they are mostly welcomed by scared people or infants. Those needles with five micro needles are called plum-blossom needles, while those with seven micro needles are called seven-star needles. Cutaneous needles are maneuvered by tapping gently the points and channels involved.

Needle Manipulation

Before acupuncture therapy is applied, all the instruments should be carefully checked and sterilized. The patient assumes one of the following positions: supine, recumbent, lateral, supine position with the knee in bent and prone positions. Most often, a patient lies supine and makes himself comfortable throughout the needling period with a pillow headrest. The acupuncturist should be alert and conscientious in the treatment procedure.

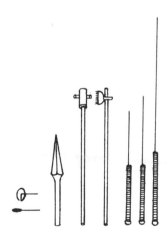

Fig. 9.10 Acupuncture needles in contemporary use

A usual practice of acupuncture is to lay the needles on the patient's body in sequences of head to bottom, proximal to distal and dorsal to ventral surfaces. The needle may be inserted into the body either vertically, horizontally or obliquely (Fig. 9.11). Vertical or perpendicular insertion is often practised on points on the limbs, back and abdomen. Points on the chest and neck are pricked obliquely while those on the face and forehead are pricked horizontally at an angle of 45 and 15 degrees respectively. The depth of insertion of a needle depends on the body build of the patient. For an average subject, half a *cun* is appropriate for points on the limbs. For safety reasons, depth of puncture should not exceed half an inch for points on the chest and much shallower for points on the head and neck.

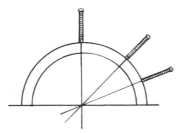

Fig. 9.11   Diagram showing the directions of acupuncture

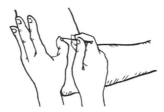

Fig. 9.12   Insertion of needle with the help of finger pressure

THE CUPPING METHOD

Cupping is a special method of treatment which is based on the principles of acupuncture. Instead of using an acupuncture needle, the acupoints derive their stimulation from suction generated by the use of a cup-shaped object. The cupping method was mentioned as early as the Jin dynasty (1115–1234 AD) in a book called *Prescriptions for Emergencies* in which ox horn was used as a cup, therefore the procedure was described as the "horn method". This primitive suction method was initially used for draining pus. Later the use was extended to the treatment of diseases caused by exogenous pathological factors and internal injuries such as *wind-cold* syndromes and the *deficiency* type of asthma. Other objects such as bamboo, earthenware cups and glassware gradually replaced ox horn for cupping. This form of therapy is often used together with acupuncture and moxibustion.

Different Types of Cups

1. *Bamboo cup*: A section of a bamboo stem, 3 to 7 cm. in diameter is cut with one end open. The cylindrical bamboo cup is then polished and shaped to various appropriate sizes.

2. *Earthenware cup:* These are made of clay or porcelain and may withstand a strong suction pressure. The shape of the cup resembles that of a drum. The drawback of earthenware cups is that they are relatively fragile.

3. *Glass cup*: The usual shape of the glass cup is a fat cup with a relatively narrow opening and a slightly inverted rim. There are different sizes for the cups. Being transparent, skin changes at the site of cupping can be monitored throughout the treatment period.

Cupping Methods

Before cupping, the site of treatment is chosen according to the principles of acupuncture. Whether the size of the cup is appropriate for the site is checked by testing the cup against the body surface. The patient should be positioned so that he/she and the practitioner are both comfortable. The rim of the cup must be free of rough edges which could cut the skin. Vaseline is put on the rim of a new cup to reduce the cupping discomfort and the danger of cutting the skin.

Negative pressure suction is created by heat which drives out the air in the cup. A simple and popular method is to place and rotate an ignited piece of alcohol-soaked cotton wool or burning paper inside the cup for several seconds. The cotton wool may then be removed. When cupping is not applied vertically, the heat source may be left inside the cup. Alcohol should not be used excessively. However, the heat should be strong enough to generate suction sufficient to hold the cup and stimulate the acupoint.

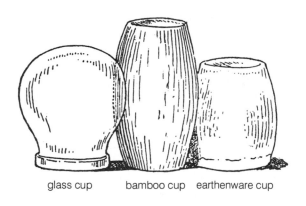

glass cup   bamboo cup   earthenware cup

Fig. 9.13   Cups used in the Cupping Method

When performing this procedure, the cup is put rapidly on the site. The negative pressure glues the cup onto the body surface. The time normally allotted for cupping is around 10 to 20 minutes, but it may be cut short if the patient cannot tolerate the suction. Freeing the cup at the end of treatment is simple. Air is leaked into the cup by pressing the skin surface down and away from the cup. Any injury of the skin inflicted in the procedure should be promptly treated and the wound should be dressed to avoid pyogenic infection. It is not unusual to find bruising at the site of cupping, but this always disappears in a few days and no treatment is required. Small scald blisters may be left alone, pending spontaneous recovery. Large blisters should be punctured under aseptic conditions and dressed with an antiseptic.

Indications and Contraindications of Cupping

Indications: *Wind cold* syndromes caused by exogenous pathogenic factors, headache, vertigo, eye pain, photophobia and aversion to light may be treated by cupping at the *Taiyang* point located at the temporal region of the skull. *Wind cold* and *damp* syndromes as well as joint pain are treated by cupping at local sites. Cupping at both sides of the back along the *Huatuojiaji* (about 1 *cun* or 1.3 inches lateral to the spinal process) helps to relieve coughs and asthma.

Contraindications: Cupping should be avoided where there is skin allergy or disease. The procedure is not practised at sites where the cup cannot be secured safely. Examples are loose skin, as in the case of emaciation, particularly bony surfaces and hairy areas. Vascular and edematous areas, ears, eyes, nose, nipples, the mouth and sensitive areas are other prohibited sites. Other contraindications of cupping include hyperpyrexia, seizures, comas, ascites, pregnancy, tumours and bleeding tendencies.

EAR ACUPUNCTURE

Ear acupuncture is a method both for the prevention and treatment of diseases by applying needles to specific areas of the ears.

According to the theory of ear acupuncture, viscera and all body parts have their own representative domain reflected on the ears. These areas have been mapped through empirical research and extensive studies. When there is a pathology in the body, certain phenomena appear in its corresponding area. These phenomena include tenderness, changes in electrical resistance or discoloration in the corresponding area. Mapping the pathology in the ears may serve as a diagnostic method to discover where the pathology is in the internal viscera. When certain stimuli are applied on these reactive regions of the ears, diseases corresponding to the body or internal organs can be cured.

Anatomy of the External Ear

The ear is essentially is a framework of cartilage wrapped with skin. The ear lobe is composed of adipose tissue underneath the skin. The nerve supply to the auricular surface comes from a complicated network of spinal and cranial nerves. The blood supply comes from the branches of the external carotid artery which has its corresponding nerves. The surface anatomy of the ear is shown in Figure 9.14.

Auricular Points

Illness in the body is reflected on certain areas or points in the ear. As mentioned briefly earlier, the pathology seen in these representative areas may be tenderness, pain, lowered electrical resistance, deformation of the auricular points, colour change, desquamation, vesicle or vascular

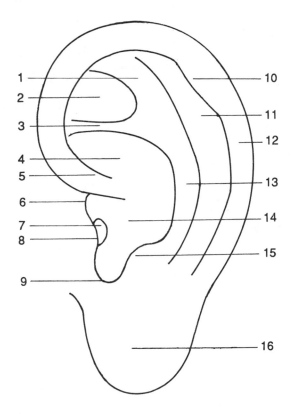

Fig. 9.14   Anatomy of the surface of the auricle

1. superior antihelix crus
2. triangular fossa
3. inferior antihelix crus
4. cymba conchae
5. helix crus
6. supratragic notch
7. orifice of external meatus
8. tragus

9. intertragic notch
10. auricular tubercle
11. scapha
12. helix
13. antihelix
14. cavum conchae
15. antitragus
16. lobule

congestion. These representative or reactive areas where changes are detectable are referred to as stimulating points for ear acupuncture, ear acupuncture points, reactive points, tender points, conducting points or sensitive points. A diagram of the representative areas of the auricle looks like an inverted fetus lying in the auricle with the head down and the feet on top.

As shown in Figure 9.15, there are quite a number of points in the auricle. The most frequently used points are listed as follows:

1. *Heart:* Located at the central depression of the concha cavity, it is mainly indicated in insomnia, dreaminess, palpitation, syncope and glossitis.

2. *Stomach:* Located in the area where the crus of helix vanishes, this point is used in digestive disorders such as ulcer pain, dyspepsia, loss of appetite, nausea and vomiting, as well as headache and insomnia.

3. *Liver:* It is located posterior to the "stomach area". The indications are for liver disease, vertigo, convulsion and oppressive fullness in the chest.

4. *Spleen:* Lateral and inferior to the "stomach area", this point is used to treat stomachaches, dyspepsia, diarrhea and muscle weakness.

5. *Lung:* The "lung area" surrounds the "heart area". Acupuncture is applied to the area in case of respiratory symptoms of a common cold, coughs and asthma as well as in cases of skin diseases such as urticaria and pruritus. It is also an important point for acupuncture analgesia.

6. *Kidney:* This point is located at the lower crus of the antihelix and right above the "heart area". The indications are for irregular menstruation, spontaneous

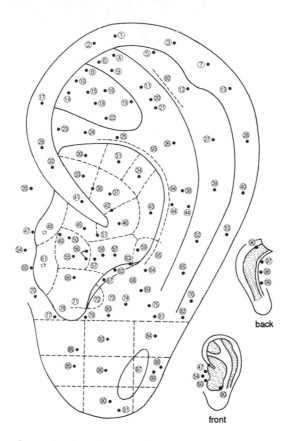

Note: ◌ indicating the points unseen from horizontal view on the inner side.

Fig. 9.15 Distribution of auricular points

① tonsil 1 ② earapix ③ liver Yang 1 ④ toe ⑤ finger ⑥ heel ⑦ helix 1
⑧ lowering blood pressure point ⑨ ankle ⑩ upper portion of the rectum ⑪ knee
joint ⑫ wrist ⑬ liver Yang 2 ⑭ external genitalia 2 ⑮ uterus ⑯ hepatitis point
⑰ external genitalia 1 ⑱ asthma point ⑲ Shenmen ⑳ hip joint ㉑ knee
㉒ femoral joint ㉓ sympathetic ㉔ sciatic nerve ㉕ buttock ㉖ abdomen
㉗ elbow ㉘ helix 2 ㉙ urethra ㉚ urinary bladder ㉛ kidney ㉜ lower portion of the
rectum ㉝ large intestine ㉞ pancreas and gall bladder ㉟ external ear
㊱ appendix ㊲ small intestine ㊳ chest ㊴ shoulder ㊵ tonsil 2 ㊶ diaphragm
㊷ duodenum ㊸ liver ㊹ mammary gland ㊺ esophagus ㊻ stomach ㊼ tragic
tip ㊽ pharynx ㊾ lower abdomen ㊿ mouth ⑤ cardiac orifice ⑤ shoulder joint
⑤ helix 3 ⑤ external nose ⑤ trachea ⑤ bronchus ⑤ lung ⑤ heart
⑤ spleen ⑥ adrenal ⑥ inner nose ⑥ brain point ⑥ brain stem ⑥ neck
⑥ clavicle ⑥ San Jiao ⑥ anti-asthma ⑥ parotid gland ⑥ occiput
⑩ hypertension point ⑪ ovary ⑫ subcortex ⑬ testis ⑭ Tai Yang ⑮ parietal
⑯ helix 4 ⑰ eye 1 ⑱ endocrine ⑲ eye 2 ⑳ forehead ㉑ lower jaw ㉒ tonsil 3
㉓ tongue ㉔ upper jaw ㉕ anesthetic point for tooth extraction ㉖ eye ㉗ face and
cheek ㉘ helix 5 ㉙ inner ear ⑨ tonsil 4 ⑨ helix 6 ⑨ urticaria area
⑨ lumbosacral vertebra ⑨ thoracic vertebra ⑨ cervical vertebra ⑨ groove for
lowering blood pressure ⑨ upper portion of the back ⑨ middle portion of the
back ⑨ lower portion of the back

seminal ejaculation, tinnitus, headache, neurosis, hearing impairment, bone fracture pain as well as diseases of the urogenital system such as nephritis and cystitis.

7. *Ear-Shenmen:* Located at the lateral one-third of the triangular fossa between the superior and inferior antihelix crus, this point regulates the functions of the cerebral cortex. The sedation effect is good for relieving anxiety and insomnia. Its analgesic action is widely applicable for the treatment of pain as well as for acupuncture analgesia.

8. *Sympathetic:* It is located at the end of flower crus of the antihelix, meeting the medial side of the helix. Acupuncture of this point relaxes the smooth muscles of the viscera and blood vessels. It is used to treat vascular spasm, spasmodic pain in the viscera, spontaneous sweating and tachycardia.

9. *Adrenal gland*: It is located at the superior medial side of the tragus, but there may be one or two divisions of the tragus. The point is at the lower one if there are two divisions as shown in the diagram. With a vascular regulatory action, it is used to relieve vascular spasm and treatment of hypertension or hypotension. The other principal indications are fever, coughs and asthma.

10. *Subcortex*: Located at the inner wall of the antitragus, this point regulates the excitation and inhibition of the cerebral cortex, and is used to treat various kinds of pain, neurasthenia, and shock.

11. *Endocrine*: Located at the foot of the incisura, it is mainly indicated in endocrine diseases such as irregular menstruation.

12. *Brainstem*: Located in the depression between the

antitragus and anthelix, this point is used to control convulsions, headaches, dizziness and vertigo.

13. *Diaphragm*: It is located at the helix crus, away from the lateral side. The indications of using this area are hemoptysis and visceral hemorrhage.

14. *Anti-asthma*: This point is located at the tip of the antitragus. If the tip of the antitragus is ambiguous, the middle point of the antitragus is used. The point has a regulatory effect on the respiratory centre. Stimulation of this point helps to attenuate asthma and to alleviate coughs and pruritus.

Searching for the Ear Points

1. *The observation method*: In the case of any ailment being present, there are unusual phenomena that will appear in specific areas of the ear. Small dark spots, tiny vesicles, white or red pimples and desquamation may be observed in the representative areas in the ear. The location of these abnormal signs is relevant to the diagnosis and treatment of diseases.

2. *The tenderness method*: The point of greatest tenderness is first ascertained, and is located somewhere near the ear point according to the ailment's location in the body. A needle head or matchstick head is used to find the most tender spot by applying light pressure on the expected reference point or the area nearby. Hitting on the most painful point, the patient will respond with feelings of discomfort or pain. If the tender point cannot be located, the ear can be massaged with the fingers and then the search resumed after a short break.

3. *The measurement of resistance of the skin*: A localized

drop in electrical resistance may occur in the auricular point corresponding to the disease. The electrical change is detectable using a cutaneous resistance meter.

Principles for Selecting the Ear Points

The careful choice of a few points is the guideline for the selection of ear points. The ear points on the ipsilateral side of the pathology are most commonly used. However, points contralateral to the pathology, or points on both sides may also be used. In order to enhance the effects of the treatment, a point may be treated with twin needles, or one needle may penetrate two points simultaneously. There are three principles involved in selecting the ear points:

1. *Selecting the points according to the corresponding locations*: The Liver point is used to treat liver diseases while the Stomach point is selected to treat a stomachache.

2. *Selecting the points according to the differentiation of syndromes in TCM*: The points are selected on the basis of the theory of meridians and collaterals and the theory of the *zang-fu* organs. According to this theory, the lung controls the skin and hair. It is evident, therefore, that the Lung point may be used to treat dermatological diseases. Similarly, the Kidney point is used to treat deafness and tinnitus. In TCM, the eye is the opening of the liver. Therefore, the Liver point may be selected for treating eye diseases.

3. *Empirical selection of points according to the special therapeutic effects of the point*: Empirical experience suggests that the Ear-*shenmen* and Sympathetic points are good for sedation and analgesia, while the Heart point is good for pain relief of a stiff neck.

Manipulation Methods of Ear Acupuncture

After locating the tender spot for acupuncture or determining the point for acupuncture, the site should be disinfected with 75% alcohol. The ear is held with the thumb close to the site of puncture with the index finger supporting the ear at the bottom. Such positioning of the ear helps to prevent the needle from penetrating through the auricle and reduces the pain of acupuncture. A sterile gauge 28 half-inch filiform needle is inserted perpendicularly into the point. Strong pain is often felt during penetration of the needle. For those with no experience of ear acupuncture, psychological support and reassurance are very important before and during the procedure.

Upon inserting the needle, the needle is twist-manipulated. It is ideal if the patient experiences a fairly strong sensation of soreness and distension. The needle is left in the ear for a period of 20 to 30 minutes and is twist-manipulated at 5 to 10 minute intervals. The painful site on the body may be massaged at the same time in order to enhance treatment. In cases of low back pain, a patient may twist his waist during the acupuncture to accelerate the analgesia. Chronic illnesses need a longer period of treatment. Up to two to three hours may be allowed for the needle to stay in situ. A dry piece of cotton wool should be ready before pulling the needle out. Hemostasis is achieved by compression with a cotton wool when there is bleeding. Ear acupuncture may be performed daily or every other day. A course of acupuncture usually comprises ten sessions.

A special variation of ear acupuncture is intradermal needling. Specially-made thumbtack needles are implanted in the acupoint and then secured in situ with adhesive plaster. This method provides sustained stimulation to a patient. Intradermal needling is especially suitable for the treatment of chronic illnesses. This method also has the advantage of convenience for a patient who is physically handicapped or too busy with work, or living far away from the hospital. A patient needs to press the needle regularly to provide stimulation. Up to seven days may be spent on each session. Complete sterilizing techniques should be respected in the procedure. Needles are removed 5 to 7 days after implantation.

Contraindications and Fainting Management

1. Ear acupuncture should not be practised in the first five months of pregnancy. For patients with a history of abortions, auricular points of the Uterus, Ovary, Endocrine and Subcortex are not to be attempted in order to avoid the risk of premature labour and abortion.

2. Nervous, hungry and tired patients should lie flat during acupuncture to reduce the risk of fainting.

3. Auricles with frostbite or infection should not be punctured, otherwise inflammation may spread in the ear. In ear acupuncture treatment, the auricle should be strictly disinfected. Any infection should be treated early with iodine or antibiotic cream to check the infection from spreading to the cartilage.

It is unusual for a patient to have fainting attacks while receiving ear acupuncture. The typical symptoms of fainting are dizziness, vertigo, pallor, sweating and low blood pressure. There is no need to pull the needle out if the symptoms are not serious. Recovery is rapid if the patient lies down, rests and tries to keep calm. A cup of warm water may be helpful. If fainting symptoms are serious, the needles should be removed immediately. Recovery may be accelerated by lifting up the lower limbs of the patient and applying auricular puncture to the Adrenal, Subcortex, Heart and Occiput auricular acupoints. Heavy pain and symptoms of dizziness, vertigo, palpitation, nausea, generalized paresthesia and cold extremities may occur during acupuncture especially when the needles are puncturing too deep or are in the wrong direction at the acupoints of the Adrenal, Sympathetic, Endocrine, Lung and Kidney. Pulling the needle slightly out often relieves the symptoms. Otherwise, the needles have to be withdrawn entirely.

Indications for Ear Acupuncture

Ear acupuncture is effective for more than just treatment of an illness. It is also useful as an analgesia and for the prevention as well as diagnosis of diseases.

Certain symptoms or manifestations of diseases may be alleviated by ear acupuncture. In an epidemic of mumps, the parotid point and Ear-*shenmen* point are punctured for disease prevention. For the prevention of seasickness, needling the Occiput point before travel is advisable.

As mentioned earlier, the auricle may show localized physical or electrical changes in the acupoint or the area which corresponds to the respective sick *zang–fu* organ. Localization of the point and relating the organ involved to the clinical presentation of the patient helps the practitioner to arrive at a diagnosis more efficiently.

The analgesic effect of ear acupuncture is often used during surgery. Simple manipulation of the needle, or passing an electric current to the acupoint through the needle can achieve an analgesic effect potent enough for operations without having to use general or regional anesthesia.

For treatment purposes, the indications of ear therapy

cover a wide range. It can treat not only many functional diseases like neurasthenia and insomnia, but also a number of organic diseases, such as inflammatory diseases and peptic ulcers. The analgesic and anti–inflammatory actions are especially remarkable. The more common indications are listed below in the following table. As this book is only an introduction to TCM, many of the points listed will be unfamiliar to the reader, and of course only experienced doctors should practise this treatment.

The Selection of Acupuncture Points for Common Ailments

Symptoms	Main points	Alternative points
1. Cough	Adrenal Gland, Lung-*Pingchuan*	Ear-*Shenmen*
2. The feeling of fullness and pain in chest	Heart, Lung, *Shenmen*	Sympathetic
3. Shortness of breath	Sympathetic, Ear-*Shenmen*, Lung	Adrenal Gland
4. Hypertension	Sympathetic, Ear-*Shenmen*, Heart	Liver
5. Heart disease	Heart, Sympathetic, Endocrine, Adrenal Gland	*Shenmen*
6. Nausea and vomiting	Stomach, Ear-*Shenmen*, Sympathetic	Subcortex
7. Stomachache	Stomach, Ear-*Shenmen*, Sympathetic	Spleen, Subcortex
8. Hiccups	Diaphragm, Ear-*Shenmen*	Subcortex
9. Indigestion	Stomach, Spleen	Endocrine
10. Diarrhea	Sympathetic, Spleen	Lung

Symptoms	Main points	Alternative points
11. Headache and vertigo	Subcortex, Brainstem	Ear-*Shenmen* Stomach
12. Insomnia	Ear-*Shenmen*, Kidney, Heart	Stomach, Subcortex
13. Stiff neck	Corresponding locations, Heart	Diaphragm, Ear-*Shenmen*
14. Pain in the joints	Corresponding locations, *Shenmen*, Adrenal Gland	Heart, Spleen
15. Frequent urination and precipitant micturition	Kidney, Ear-*Shenmen*	Subcortex, Sympathetic
16. Menorrhagia	Endocrine, Ear-*Shenmen*	Kidney, Sympathetic
17. Menstrual disorders	Endocrine, Ear-*Shenmen*	Spleen, Kidney
18. Sore throat	Heart, Lung	Endocrine, Adrenal Gland
19. Eye diseases	Corresponding locations, Liver	Spleen, Kidney
20. Dermatosis	Corresponding locations, Lung, Ear-*Shenmen*, Endocrine	Adrenal Gland
21. First-aid (heat-stroke, shock)	Subcortex, Adrenal Gland, Heart	Sympathetic, Brainstem

HYDRO-ACUPUNCTURE

Hydro-acupuncture therapy or liquid-acupuncture therapy is a form of treatment combining both acupuncture and drugs. Drugs used for intramuscular administration are injected into the acupuncture point or tender point to achieve the desired effect. This method exploits the efficacies of both acupuncture and the pharmacological actions of the drug being used.

Therapeutic Methods

The site of injection varies according to the type of disease and the goal of treatment.

1. *Injection at the tender spot*: This method is often quoted in cases of soft tissue injury, such as muscle pain in the back or limbs, shoulder pain and pain due to sprains and contusions of the joints and soft tissues. It may also be effective in the treatment of a prolapsed intervertebral disc and tendosynovitis. The injection site is the point where tenderness is most obvious on palpation.

    Tender spots are most often found on both sides in the spinal muscles at the level of the fourth and fifth lumbar vertebrae and lateral to the posterior superior iliac spine and sacroiliac joint. In patients with knee pain, tender spots are usually found in the soft tissues of the lateral compartments above and around the joint. In case of shoulder pain, the spots are located in the soft tissue around the shoulder joint.

2. *Point-injection*: The principle of point-injection is similar to that of acupuncture. Injection may also be applied to points used in ear acupuncture.

Frequently Used Drugs and Their Dosages

Drugs which may be easily absorbed and have a stimulating effect on the acupoint, but have little or no side effects are used. To enhance the effects of the treatment, the drug normally chosen for the particular illness may be used for injection into the acupoint. A dextrose solution (5 to 10%) or a procaine hydrochloride (0.5–1%) solution is often used in a volume of 15 to 20 millilitres. Other ingredients such as vitamin B1 (50–100 mg) may be added. Chinese angelica (3–5% solution), vitamin B1, B12, antibiotics, atropine, chlorpromazine and paniculate swallowwort root solutions may also be injected in a volume of 0.2–2 millilitres.

Injection apparatus is the same as that used for an intramuscular injection. After being selected, the site of injection is disinfected with alcohol. The needle is inserted the same as in performing acupuncture, and is then manipulated by lifting and pushing to achieve the effect of "the arrival of *qi*". When the patient has a sensation of numbness or soreness, mild suction is applied to the syringe to ensure that no blood comes out and that the syringe is not hitting a blood vessel. Then the drug is pushed into the acupoint. A rapid push is required for injection at the tender spot while a slow push is more suitable for injection at the acupoint.

For large–dose injections, which cause a stronger stimulation of the tender spot, treatment should be done on alternate days or twice weekly. Daily or alternate day treatment may be required for small–dose injections. The course of treatment depends on the progress of the disease. The usual course is 10 days with a rest of 5–7 days in between.

Precautions of Hydrotherapy

1. Penetration of the needle at sites on the chest and at the back must be superficial and light. Too deep an injection runs the risk of inducing pneumothorax. The usual depth is about half a *cun*. However the depth varies with each patient. Superficial injection is practised when there is tenderness on light palpation of the superficial tissue. On the contrary, a deeper injection is required for pathology at a deeper level, as suggested by tenderness elicited only by deep palpation.

2. Injection at the sacral acupoints is prohibited in pregnancy. Elderly patients should not receive too many injections and the dose of the drug should be appropriately adjusted.

3. It is important not to inject drugs into a joint cavity when the acupoint is located nearby, otherwise there may be inflammatory reactions such as fever, swelling, redness and pain. Without complications, these symptoms will subside spontaneously in 2 to 3 days.

4. Aseptic techniques are essential in hydrotherapy. Septic signs such as local erythema, swelling and pain should be promptly treated. Mild discomfort at the site of injection is not unusual 4 to 8 hours after injection. The discomfort may last for a few hours to a day. Hydrotherapy is thus most comfortably administered every other day.

5. Do not twist the syringe after it is inserted. Light lifting and pushing provide good enough stimulation.

6. Any drug that the patient is allergic to is contraindicated. Specific enquiries of drug allergies (e.g. penicillin) are essential prior to injection of drug.

Common Diseases Treated with Hydro-acupuncture Therapy

Hydrotherapy is useful in the treatment of a large variety of diseases. The indications are essentially the same as those of acupuncture. The most common indications are as follows:

1. *Liver diseases* (including chronic hepatitis, protracted hepatitis, cirrhosis of the liver): The frequently used acupuncture points are *Yanglingquan* (G 34) and *Zusanli* (S 36). Common injection solutions are PROHEPARIN and Vitamin B12.

2. *Stomach diseases* (including gastric arthritis, digestive ulcer, etc.): Frequently used acupuncture points are *Weishu* (B 21), *Pishu* (B 20), *Zusanli* (S 36) and *Sanyinjiao* (Sp 6). Injection solution is Vitamin B1 or Vitamin B complex.

3. *Asthma*: Acupuncture points like *Feishu* (B 13) and *Dachangshu* (B 25) may be used. Vitamin B1 is one of the injection solutions.

4. *Fever*: Acupuncture points like *Quchi* (LI 11) on both sides may be used. Injection solution used is 0.2 millilitre of analgin.

5. *Neurasthenia*: Frequently used acupuncture points are *Sanyinjiao* (Sp 6) and *Zusanli* (S 36). Injection solution is 1 to 2 millilitres of 0.5% procaine.

6. *Pain syndromes*: such as low back pain, frozen shoulder, sciatica, arthritis of the knee and spinal hypertrophy may be treated by injection at the localized tender points. Frequently used drugs are Angelica Sinensis, safflower (Flos Carthami), clematis root (Radix Clematidis) preparations or a 5–10% glucose solution.

Contraindications for
Acupuncture and Moxibustion

Acupuncture is not indicated in a patient who is thirsty, hungry, drunk, overfed, exhausted, angry, frightened or depressed. Extra care should be paid to pregnant women. Acupoints in the lower abdomen and the sacral region should not be attempted in the first five months of pregnancy. Out of absolute necessity, acupuncture applied to these points should be light and strong manipulation is prohibited. Beyond the first five months, points at the upper abdomen and lateral sides should also be avoided. Acupoints closely related to the genital system, such as *Sanyinjiao* (Sp 6), *Hegu* (LI 4) and *Shenshu* (U 23) are contraindicated for the potential danger of abortion or premature labour. The increased risk of mishap of pregnancy and even intrauterine death might in fact be attributed to fainting reaction during acupuncture when fetal blood circulation and oxygen supply are jeopardized.

Fainting reaction during acupuncture has similar deleterious effect on patients with hyperpyrexia complicating infectious disease. The thermoregulation of the central nervous system may be upset and the body temperature may rise dangerously high. Acupuncture is therefore not recommended in case of hyperpyrexia.

Diseases which require surgical intervention, severe infectious diseases, or organic diseases which require specific treatment (e.g. cirrhosis, bone fracture, scurvy, bleeding esophageal varices) should not be treated primarily with acupuncture. Indiscriminate use of acupuncture would delay appropriate treatment and jeopardize the patient. Direct puncture of a malignant tumor accelerates metastasis and hence acupuncture is contraindicated at the site of a tumor.

Acupuncture is uncomfortable and undesirable in

sensitive areas such as the lips, nipples, fingertips and perineum. Fainting reaction is more likely in neurotic and weak patients. Special caution against traumatic bleeding is important when the location of an acupoint is close to a blood vessel (*Weizhong*, B 40; *Jimai*, Liv 12). Otherwise severe diathesis or thrombosis may occur. Acupuncture points near vital organs like *Xinhui* (GV 22), Tanzhong (CV 17), *Ruzhong* (S 17) and *Qimen* (Liv 14) are contraindicated or not to be punctured deeply for the potential danger of damage to vital organs such as the cerebrum, heart and liver. The *Shenque* (CV 8) point at the umbilicus is difficult to disinfect and is just superficial to the peritoneal cavity. Puncture of the point is prohibited and only moxibustion should be avoided.

Ordinary moxa cones can generate a skin temperature of 50°C. The heat penetrates deep under the skin. The nerve and muscle underneath may lose their activity at a temperature of 45°C. Hence moxibustion should be cautiously applied or prohibited at acupoints superficial to major nerve trunks. For example, under the acupuncture point *Ermen* (TE 21) is the facial nerve. *Zanzhu* (B 2) is located near the supratrochlear nerve. Deep to the *Chengfu* (B 36) is the sciatic nerve while under the *Biguan* (S 31) is the femoral nerve. Old TCM literature warned against moxibustion at all these acupuncture points.

APPENDIX:
Modern Research on the
Mechanism of Acupuncture Analgesia

The success of acupuncture analgesia created extensive interest in this field both in China and overseas. Since the nineteen-sixties, research has been going on studying the mechanism of acupuncture analgesia. Preliminary research showed that the body fluids contain analgesic ingredients induced by acupuncture. Cross blood transfusion of two rabbits revealed that analgesia induced by acupuncture is transferable to the recipient rabbit. Analgesia was also transferable to a recipient animal by cross perfusion of the cerebral ventricle with artificial cerebrospinal fluid of the donor receiving acupuncture. Subsequent research showed that chemicals such as acetylcholine, catecholamine, 5-hydroxytryptamine (5-HT), enkephalins and endorphins are the mediators of analgesia.

Extensive animal experiments showed that the 5-HT concentration in the central nervous system increased in parallel with the analgesic effect induced by acupuncture. On the other hand the concentration of acetylcholine after acupuncture is inconsistent. Most reports showed that the activities of acetylcholine and cholinesterase were increased in the caudate nuclei and hypothalamus, which implies that analgesia might be closely related to cholinergic nerve supply to these two areas.

Another neurotransmitter playing a significant role in acupuncture analgesia is the catecholamines. In animal experiments, the norepinephrine content in the brain was lowered after acupuncture. Haloperidol, a dopamine receptor inhibitor, is now used to enhance the analgesic effect of acupuncture in thyroidectomy.

In 1975, enkephalins carrying the activity of morphine were isolated from brain tissues in the periaqueductal grey and diencephalon. Other opiate substances, such as the endorphins from the hypothalamus and pituitary gland, dynorphin and substance P, were found to be playing a significant role in analgesia induced by acupuncture. Substantial experimental evidence showed that in acupuncture-induced analgesia the pain threshold was raised in parallel with increasing activity of enkephalins in midbrain and anterior cerebrum. A delayed degradation of endorphin was associated with prolonged period of analgesia. After repeated acupuncture, tolerance of endorphin effect occurred. Despite rising concentration of endorphin in the central nervous system, the analgesic effect not only failed to increase, but was on the contrary found to be decreasing. This tolerance of acupuncture analgesia and endorphin accords with the tolerance of morphia's pain-killing action. An in vivo inhibiter of endorphin has been isolated from the brain of rats which developed tolerance of acupuncture. Injection of the inhibitor extract into the cerebral ventricle of another rat induced similar tolerance against acupuncture and morphine analgesia in the recipient animal.

Other than the neurochemical basis, the mechanism of acupuncture analgesia has also been explored on electrophysiological terms. A large number of experimental studies have been carried out in China on the neural mechanism of acupuncture. There were good evidences of acupuncture blocking the afferent and efferent pathways of pain transmission in the nervous system. Pain signals as perceived by the peripheral pain receptors travel along the sensory nerve fibres to the dorsal horn of the spinal cord where they are transmitted to the ventrobasal complex of the thalamus in the ascending afferent pathway comprising essentially the dorsolateral tract and ventrolateral tract of the spinal cord and medial lemniscus. The pain sensation is then discriminated and projected anatomically at the level of the cerebral cortex. On the other hand, cognition of pain is affected by a wide variety of factors such as anxiety and attention. The interaction of pain perception is supposed to come from the cortex and higher centres of the brain influencing pain transmission in the afferent conduction system. This is known as the efferent inhibition of pain. Under normal circumstances, the gate theory suggests that perception of pain signal is inhibited by signals coming from non-pain receptors. The exact mechanism has not been entirely worked out yet. Acupuncture provides counter-stimulation of the non-pain receptors jamming the pain signal transmission. This is analogous to closing the gate of pain signal transmission at either the afferent or the efferent pathway.

Research on the mechanism by which acupuncture works is still continuing. Histochemical, electrophysiological and immunochemical methods have been utilized to put on details of the mechanism of acupuncture. More and more neurochemical transmitters have been identified and evaluated for their action and interaction with other neurotransmitters. Readers are encouraged to refer to recent literature from professional journals of pain research and acupuncture. An excellent review of the topic is Lu Gwei-Djen and Joseph Needham's book: *Celestial Lancets— A History and Rationale of Acupuncture and Moxa.*

10

TUI-NA THERAPY

Tui-na is a special form of massage therapy using only a pair of hands. No drug or special equipment is required. The method of massage depends on the pattern and severity of a disease.

The TCM method of *tui-na* is quite different from ordinary massage. It is a special form of treatment developed from ancient massage techniques. In contrast to simple massage, which is an auxiliary therapy, *tui-na* is used as the primary method of treatment, and is based on the theories and basic principles of TCM. The concept of the meridians, the four diagnoses and the eight principal syndromes are the guidelines of diagnosis and treatment. Within this discipline, the theory of the meridians is of paramount importance, because both the type of therapy and choice of acupoints depend on the meridian involved.

Basic Manipulations

Tui-na is a kind of rhythmic massage on a patient's body. There are more than twenty variations of these manipulations, the most common of which are: (1) pushing, (2) grabbing, (3) pressing, (4) round-rubbing, (5) rubbing, (6) rotating; (7) kneading, (8) tapping, (9) rolling, (10) chiropractic along the spine. The application of manipulations is related to the site of the pathology, the severity of the disease as well as personal practice and experience. The manipulation methods may vary according to the practising clinician. Nevertheless, they all aim at the same goal of providing a gentle, forceful and sustained stimulation penetrating into the deeper tissue.

A brief description of the ten commonly used basic manipulations and their effects is given below:

(1) Pushing

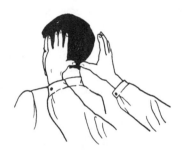

Fig. 10.1   Pushing manipulation

The finger, palm or elbow are used to provide a pushing force on a specific location or acupoint. The force used is moderate and acts on a comparatively small area. Pushing is applicable to all acupuncture points on the body, but is most often used on the head, chest, abdomen and the joints of the four limbs. It has the function of relaxing the muscles and activating the flow of *qi* and *blood* in the meridians as well as invigorating the spleen and stomach. Hence, the pushing method is used on patients with headaches, abdominal pain and joint pain.

(2) Grabbing

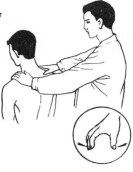

Fig. 10.2
Grabbing manipulation

There are two variations of grabbing. The first one, called "turnaround grabbing", involves gripping the muscle and rocking it to and fro. The other method is called "pinch grabbing", by which the muscle is massaged with alternating grabbing and relaxing movements. This provides a strong stimulation to the massage site and serves to expel *wind*, to clear away the *cold* and to relax the muscles and tendons. Grabbing is often used in the treatment of spasmodic pain in the neck, shoulders, back and on the four limbs.

(3) Pressing (including spot manipulation and squeezing)

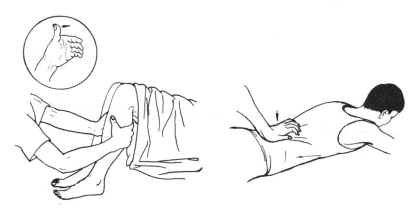

Fig. 10.3   Pressing manipulations

The thumb or root of the palm is applied to the site with increasing force by twisting and twirling.

There is little difference in the techniques of pressing and spotting. Both achieve relaxation of the muscles, relief of pain, and the correction of spinal deformities. These methods are often practised for the treatment of pain and numbness of the limbs, scoliosis and abdominal pain.

Fig. 10.4   Spot manipulation

(4) Rubbing

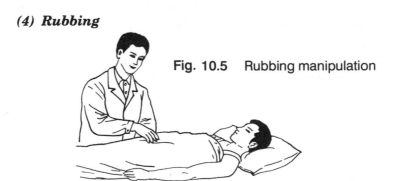

Fig. 10.5   Rubbing manipulation

The patient is rubbed with the palm or fingertip on the treatment site, using a rhythmic rotating force through the wrist and forearm. The stimulation is mild and soft. Rubbing is often practised on the chest, abdomen and costal areas. It regulates *qi* in the middle *jiao*, regulates gut motility and facilitates digestion so that dyspepsia and bloating due to indigestion are relieved.

(5) *Round-rubbing*

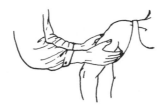

Fig. 10.6   Round-rubbing manipulation

As shown in the figure above, the site being massaged is held in between the palms and is rubbed strongly and quickly with an up and down movement. The manoeuver promotes the flow of *qi* and *blood* in the channels and collaterals and relaxes the muscles. Round-rubbing is often used before the end of a *tui-na* session.

(6) *Rotating*

Holding the proximal and distal parts of the limbs, the affected joint is rotated gently, as shown in the figure below. The manipulation mobilizes the joint, relaxes the ligaments and breaks down adhesions in the synovium.

This method is thus often practised on the neck and lumbar areas, and on large joints in cases of stiffness, contractures and spasticity.

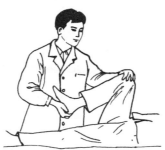

Fig. 10.7   Rotating manipulation

(7) Kneading

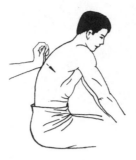

Fig. 10.8　Kneading manipulation

Without leaving the acupoint, a rotating force is applied gently through the thumb.

Kneading should be done in a light and slow manner. It relieves tightness of the chest and regulates the flow of *qi*. The massage accelerates the resolution of swelling and pain. Hence kneading is often used to relieve abdominal pain or distension, pain in the chest or hypochondrium, constipation, edema and pain.

(8) Tapping

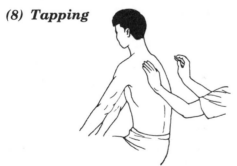

Fig. 10.9
Tapping manipulation

Either one or both hands are used to tap gently and rhythmically on the site receiving treatment. Tapping increases regional blood circulation, relieves muscle fatigue, cramps and spasms. This technique is often used to treat paresthesia, pain and muscle spasms in the shoulder, the lumbar areas and lower limbs.

(9) *Rolling*

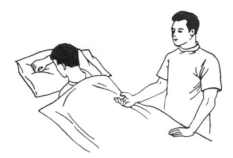

Fig. 10.10 Rolling manipulation

The dorso-lateral rim of the hand is laid on the site receiving treatment and a rolling force is applied through a rotating movement of the wrist. This allows a heavier force to be applied on a wider surface area and hence may be used on the shoulder, the back, the limbs and the lumbar or gluteal areas where the muscles are thick. The rolling technique relaxes muscle spasms and activates the flow of blood. This method finds its application in the treatment of rheumatic pain, numbness and muscular injuries.

Other miscellaneous *tui-na* techniques include pulling and stepping methods. The former involves pulling the limbs in opposite directions to break down adhesions of muscles and ligaments or to correct deformities of the spine or skeleton. The latter method requires stepping on the site needing treatment using one or both feet. This is most often practised on patients for the correction of spinal deformities and for relieving pain due to prolapsed intervertebral discs. These methods should be reserved for experienced experts who have acquired special skills that are quite beyond the scope of this book.

(10) Chiropractic along the spine

(A) Hand posture

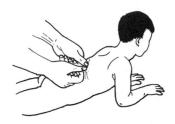

(B) Kneading the muscles along the spine

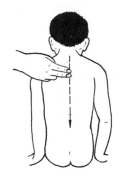

(C) Pushing along the spine

Fig. 10.11   Massaging along the spine

Tui-na along the spine may also be practised in the pediatric age group for treating certain diseases. The younger the child is (usually under 5 years old), the more effective *tui-na* will be. The basic techniques are similar to those for adults. However, manipulations are much softer and gentler in order not to injure the child. Ginger extract, alcohol or a lubricant may be applied onto the skin before the commencement of *tui-na* to enhance the comfort and effectiveness of *tui-na* therapy. More gentle techniques should be practised first so that the child does not become apprehensive of the procedure. There are two special skills specifically practised on children:

1. *Treatment by kneading the muscles along the spine with the fingers*: Along both sides of the spine, the skin is pinched up with the thumbs and index fingers of both hands, massaged and then released immediately. The manipulation continues with rhythmic coordination of both hands travelling distally from the sacral area to the caudal *Dazhui* (GV 14) area. Both sides of the spine should be worked. Spinal kneading is often used to treat anorexia, malnutrition and indigestion in children.

2. *Pushing along the spine*: With the index and middle fingers of both hands held together, the spine is pushed and rubbed along the mid-line from the *Dazhui* (GV 14) point distally to the sacral area (Fig. 10.11c). This manipulation helps to bring down high fevers.

Precautions of *Tui-na*

Practitioners should keep their fingernails short in order

not to scratch the skin of the patient. In winter, as one might expect, practitioners should keep their hands as warm as possible when doing treatment, for the comfort of the patients. A patient may rest after *tui-na* treatment if the procedure is felt to be tiring.

Indications and Contraindications

Indications: Stiff neck, back pain, spinal and muscular injury, frozen shoulder, prolapsed intervertebral disc, sciatica, headache, epigastric pain, gastroptosis, insomnia and infantile malnutrition (*deficiency* syndrome of the kidney and stomach).

Contraindications: *Tui-na* therapy should in no cases be applied on the abdomen, iliac and lumbo-sacral regions of pregnant women or during their menstrual period. Neither should it be applied to locations where there is bleeding, infection or skin diseases. *Tui-na* is also contraindicated in bone injuries, pyogenic infections and tuberculosis.

11

QIGONG THERAPY

Qigong therapy is a special method used for treating and preventing diseases, as well as for maintaining good health. It is also called *internal* exercise as it directs its effects on the *internal zang-fu* organs.

Qigong, like *tui-na*, also finds its theoretical basis in the fundamental concepts of TCM and in the meridian theory of acupuncture. In the *Nei Jing*, it is stated that concentration of the mind and one's essence on the *internal* (*zang-fu*) organs keeps disease away. To achieve this goal, the practice of *qigong* starts with breathing exercises. Through coordinated breathing, one attains a mental serenity which may increase the resistance of the body to disease. Practised over a period of time, it may even heal local pathologies. Hence, *qigong* is a type of exercise that promotes good health through a holistic approach of the mind and body.

The *qi* of *qigong* is the same *qi* we have discussed at length in this book, and the *gong* means "skill", or "the practice of a skill". Thus the word *qigong* means the skill of training and controlling one's *qi*. Training in *qigong* is aimed at two essential elements, the *qi* and the mind.

The Training of *Qi*

Qi refers to both the breath and the circulating *qi* in the body. In contrast to ordinary sports training, *qigong* emphasizes breathing using the abdomen rather than the chest. There are three different types of abdominal breathing. In "normal sequence breathing", the abdomen distends on inhalation and contracts on exhalation. The reverse is true for "reverse sequence breathing". In the third type of "latent breathing", the abdominal movement is minimal and the breathing movement is extremely smooth and soft. Though the skills of these three breathing exercises are different, they share a common basic principle: the breathing should always be natural, soft and smooth.

Control of one's breathing is essential in the practice of *qigong*. The practice of these breathing techniques is a means by which the balance and functioning of the *internal zang-fu* organs are reinforced. How to train the body to make good use of the *internal energy* is more important than the breathing itself. *Qi* refers not only to a breath of air, but also the *qi* circulating in the body, a sensation of flowing air which can actually be felt during the practice of *qigong*. The use of these breathing exercises strengthens the *internal qi* and *blood* as well as regulating their flow within the meridian system. In the process of doing these exercises, the body and mind attain a serenity which enables the flow of *qi* to be felt. *Qi* stimulates and regulates the functions of the *zang-fu* organs, which are governed by the specific channels along which the *qi* flows. Activation of the meridian system through *qigong* thereby promotes the healthy functioning of the essential *zang-fu* organs. The practice of *qigong* begins from the Conception Vessel and Governor Vessel meridians (see Chapter 9 on Acupuncture). Through the eight extra-meridians, the circulation of *qi* and *blood* is activated in the twelve channels to promote the harmony of the whole *zang-fu* system.

Learning how to perform abdominal breathing is essential in *qigong* exercise. The abdomen is the engine of both *qi* and *blood*. After a brief period of doing the breathing and mind concentration, a flow of heat or a sensation of the actual *qi* may be experienced in the abdomen. The *qi* sensation may be directed from the lower abdomen to the caudal end of the spine and then upwards along the spine to the vertex. The flow of *qi* may then be directed downwards anteriorly through the head and trunk back to the lower abdomen where the *qi* flow begins. This is how *qi* goes around the Conception Vessel and Governor Vessel meridians.

The Training of the Mind

The flow of *qi* is under the direct control of the mind. How to concentrate the mind to invigorate the *qi* effectively is of paramount importance in the practice of *qigong*, otherwise the flow of *qi* cannot be felt and reinforced. Distraction of the mind, in the beginning at least, is virtually inevitable. However, distraction should be kept to a minimum in order to sublimate the mind to a "serene state". It may be easy not to be distracted. A simple and often effective way is to keep on reminding oneself not to think of anything while practising *qigong*. Another simple method is to concentrate on the breathing exercise and counting the breaths. If these simple procedures fail, one may stop and relax for a while before continuing. Struggling too hard to relax the mind is not advisable, as it may only result in tensing up parts of the body.

There are three important principles in *qigong* practice—physical and mental relaxation, coordination of the mind and *qi* and finally the rhythm of the practice. The first principle refers to the relaxation of the muscles of the whole body. Physical relaxation must be attained before relaxation of the mind be accomplished. It may not be easy to relax the whole body physically, but after a certain amount of practice, anyone can master this task. One's achievement and progress should be as natural as possible, without forcing the body or the mind. Serenity of the mind means calming one's thoughts, as in meditation, and is quite different from the mental state of sleep. Unlike the latter, the mind has to focus on something, such as the breathing exercises in *qigong*, and not allow other distractions to interfere in the practice.

Good coordination between the mind and *qi* is the second principle of *qigong*. Breathing should never be forceful but as smooth and soft as possible. The action should be natural and under the direction of the mind. For beginners of *qigong*, it is important that they do not drag out their breath for too long. *Qigong* is more than a breathing exercise. Only when the breath is under control of the mind can it be long and deep. When the mind coordinates well with the breathing, automatically the breaths will be soft, deep and steady, not tense, uncomfortable and unsteady.

The third principle of *qigong* reminds us as to when and how to rest during practice. Every now and then, and also near the end of doing *qigong*, one should exhale and hold the breath in the lower abdomen for a while. The mind should be totally blank for a few minutes, entering a twilight state similar to but not entirely the same as the sleep state. This pattern of alternating breathing and resting saves the energy of a patient and enables *qigong* to be practised for a longer period of time.

The *Qigong* Methods

The Relaxation Method

One should lie supine with the legs stretched out (Fig. 11.1). The toes should point upwards and both hands should lie flat on the sides of the body. Both the eyes and the mouth should be lightly closed. The whole body should be relaxed. Inhale with the nose and then exhale through the mouth slowly and steadily. The mind should be kept relaxed throughout. It may not be possible to relax the whole body at the same time. Try to relax parts of the body first. There is no fixed priority as to which part of the body should be relaxed first. If the head and facial muscles cannot be relaxed, then attempt should be directed to somewhere else such as the limbs. It is not necessary trying to relax the whole body in one cycle of breathing. In the first breath cycle, part of the body may be relaxed. Usually, the process of relaxation becomes easier to accomplish in the following breath cycles. After several breathing cycles, the whole body and the mind should become relaxed and serene without any preoccupations of distracting thoughts. Each session should last from about 10 to 20 minutes.

Fig. 11.1   The supine posture

The relaxation method is often practised in preparation for practising other *qigong* procedures. It may also be practised alone as a means of relieving tension from work or daily life. The relaxation method is also good for inducing a good night's sleep and relieving hypertension and mild bronchial asthma.

The Healing Qigong

Practice of this method has a healing effect. There are two different postures that may be used to practise this technique.

1. *The lying posture*: The patient should lie laterally on the bed with the head resting comfortably on a pillow in a slightly flexed position. Both the eyes and the mouth should be loosely and effortlessly closed. The hand on top is stretched out comfortably and is placed on the hip joint. The hand on the ventral side faces upward, slightly scooped and is placed about 2 inches from the head. The spine is slightly hyperextended. The leg underneath is stretched out comfortably and mildly flexed at the knee. The leg on top is bent at a right angle and rests on the other leg (Fig. 11.2).

Fig. 11.2 Lying on one side

2. *The sitting posture*: The subject sits on a stool whose height allows the knees to assume a right angle. The whole body should be totally relaxed. Both hands are put on the thighs, close to the knees. The legs are opened at the hips until they are in line with the shoulders. Both the eyes and mouth are gently closed. The chest should be slightly flexed but not hyperextended. Both shoulder joints should be relaxed with the upper limbs hanging loosely and vertically.

Fig. 11.3
Normal sitting posture

Training of the mind begins with the clearing of distracting thoughts, after assuming the correct posture. Attention of the mind should be focused on a spot called the *dantian*, which is located 5 cm.(or 2 inches) below the belly-button. Air is exhaled through the nose with the abdomen contracting and the tongue lying on the floor of the mouth. In the inhalation phase, the abdomen distends and the tip of the tongue touches the hard palate. Saliva secreted during breathing may be swallowed slowly. Focusing the mind on the *dantian* helps one's concentration and allows one not to be easily distracted when practising *qigong*. The key points of *qigong* practice are keeping the mind relaxed and having coordinated abdominal breathing. Otherwise, the mind and *qi* cannot attain harmony and achieve the goals of *qigong* practice.

The method using the lying posture is more comfortable for weak patients. However, patients may doze or fall asleep in this posture and hence defeat the purpose of *qigong* practice. The abdominal breathing stimulates the appetite and metabolism of the body. Through calming of the mind, *qigong* lessens the severity of diseases related to the sympathetic system such as ulcer diseases and neurosis. Owing to stimulation of one's bowels, abdominal distension during breathing is not emphasized for patients suffering from diarrhea. Each session should last for approximately 20 to 30 minutes.

Strengthening Qigong

This method not only has certain healing effects, but also enhances the general health of the subject. There are also two positions possible when practising this method.

1. *The sitting posture*: There are three variations of this posture. The first one is the comfortable sitting posture (Fig. 11.4). The subject sits comfortably with both legs crossed. The second method is to cross the right leg on top of the left or vice versa according to individual preference (Fig. 11.5). The last variation is twisting both left and right legs over each other, with the surfaces of both feet turned slightly upwards (Fig. 11.6).

Fig. 11.4   Natural cross-legged posture

Fig. 11.5   Single cross-legged posture

Fig. 11.6   Double cross-legged posture

In all of the sitting postures, the hips should be square. The spine should be straight without hyperextension in a natural and relaxed position so that the chest and pectoral girdle will neither protrude nor collapse. The hands are positioned in front of the abdomen with the thumbs crossing each other and the fingers of one hand lying on top of those of the other. The hands may also be put prone on the thighs. Both eyes are loosely closed. The twisting posture is relatively difficult to sustain. It is usual to start with a comfortable sitting posture and leave the most difficult method until last in *qigong* training.

2. *The standing posture* (Fig. 11.7): The subject stands comfortably with the feet 5 inches apart. The heels are turned out at an angle of about 45 degrees. The hands are open in such a way that the fingers are slightly separated and bent as if one is holding a ball. The upper limbs assume a circular posture along the plane of the shoulders as if holding a tree. Both knees are slightly flexed. The dorsal spine should be kept in the natural position so that it is neither hyperextended nor hyperflexed. The centre of gravity will then fall in between the legs. The eyes are loosely closed.

Fig. 11.7   The "three rounds" standing posture

The breathing and concentration of the mind are essentially the same as mentioned earlier. Breathing may be soft and natural, or steady and deep. Either the "normal sequence" or the "reversed sequence" abdominal breathing method may be used.

The strengthening method of *qigong* is good for patients recovering from *deficiency* syndromes and debilitating diseases. It is also indicated in hypertension and neurosis. The standing posture also strengthens the legs, spine, arms and wrists and the soft tissues in the respective regions.

The Health-Promoting Qigong

This is a *qi* conduction therapy discovered long ago in ancient China. The relaxation and mind control are coordinated with certain exercises of the body to achieve a harmony of active (or external) and passive (or internal) movements. Health-promoting *qigong* is best practised on a bed in a sitting position with the legs crossed. There are eight different types of exercises that can be practised, each with its unique effects.

1. *Hitting of the head and teeth*: The upper maxillary teeth should rest lightly and tap on those of the lower mandibular set. With both ears covered by the palms, the occiput of the head is tapped repeatedly from up to down with the tips of the first and middle fingers. The patient will hear a sound similar to a drum being hit. This method is good for strengthening the teeth and the prevention of dental illnesses, as well as for relieving headaches, dizziness and vertigo.

Fig. 11.8
Hitting of the head and teeth

2. *The turning left and right movement*: The subject looks at the shoulder while turning the neck left and right. This is good for the neck and syndromes of the spleen and stomach.

Fig. 11.9
Turning the head and neck left and right

3. *The salivation method*: With the tip of the tongue touching the upper palate, the teeth lightly grind each other in a rotating movement. The saliva secreted in the procedure is not swallowed but is saved in the mouth. Rinsing the oral cavity for a while, the saliva is swallowed slowly in three small separate mouthfuls under the direction of the mind focusing from the mouth downwards to the *dantian*. This prevents bitterness in the mouth and throat diseases, and promotes digestion.

4. *The lumbar massage*: After vigorous rubbing, the hands thus warmed are put on the loin area at the back and massage is then performed. Repeat the massage twenty-four times each turn. This manoeuvre prevents low back pain and dysmennorhea.

Fig. 11.10
The lumbar massage

5. *The left-and-right stretch*: Fully stretch both arms to the left and right with the hands in a fist as if pulling on something. Repeat twelve times each turn. This procedure helps to maintain good posture.

Fig. 11.11
The left-and-right stretch

6. *Rotating of the shoulder and arm*: Both shoulders and arms are rotated together alternately like wheels. Practise the rotations twenty-four times each turn. This helps to reinforce the functions of the *zang-fu* organs.

Fig. 11.12
Rotating of the shoulder and arm

7. *The up-down lifting sequence*: Rest both hands on the knees and then lift one arm up above the head. The palms should face upward and the wrists should be flexed. The mind should be in a state of meditation, concentrating on the image of supporting the sky with one's hands. In the lifting procedure, the eyes follow the hand. Both upper limbs alternate the practice twenty-four times. This manoeuvre promotes the healthy functioning of the spleen and stomach to aid digestion and the assimilation of nutrients.

Fig. 11.13　The up-down lifting sequence

8.　*The leg stretch*: Sitting on a bed, both feet are stretched out as far as possible, twenty-four times. This stretches stiff legs and promotes the circulation of blood.

Fig. 11.14　The leg stretch

Precautions of *Qigong* Practice

1.　The environment in which *qigong* is practised should be calm. Good ventilation is essential for breathing exercises. Polluted air and dust should be avoided. It is recommended to also stay away from windy areas.

2.　Before beginning a *qigong* exercise, the bladder and bowel should preferably be emptied first. A cup of water quenches the thirst and helps nervous subjects to calm down. Tight clothing, belts and buttons should be loosened in order to free the circulation of *qi* and blood.

3.   At the end of *qigong* practice, open the eyes slowly and massage the face and upper limbs with both hands that have been warmed from rubbing. Rise up slowly and gradually resume normal activities.

4.   Sexual activity is discouraged, especially for those who have a weak physique, during the period of treatment.

5.   It is not advisable to be obsessive in achieving rapid progress in *qigong*. Practice of *qigong* should follow a steady ongoing program, especially for those patients still in rehabilitation from an illness. Over-enthusiastic practice of *qigong* may result in fatigue. The usual program is to practise *qigong* twice or three times a day, each session lasting about 20 minutes. *Qigong* practice should not start immediately after eating. An hour and a half rest after eating is recommended, and the patient should be careful not to overeat.

6.   Book knowledge alone is not sufficient for good *qigong* training. Advice and coaching from a tutor is very important. *Qigong* brings a feeling of relaxation and elation to a person. However, beginners may experience myalgia if they fail to relax the muscles in the body. Inappropriate or over-intensive breathing exercise may cause chest pain or tightness. If one is unable to concentrate the mind and achieve mental serenity, *qigong* may be stopped and tried again shortly afterwards.

Indications and Contraindications

Qigong is indicated for the treatment or the lessening of the symptoms of the following diseases:

1. Cardiovascular diseases: hypertension, rheumatic heart disease.

2. Respiratory diseases: tuberculosis, bronchial asthma, emphysema, silicosis.

3. Digestive diseases: gastric and duodenal ulcer, chronic gastritis, chronic hepatitis, early liver cirrhosis.

4. Endocrine diseases: diabetes, thyrotoxicosis.

5. Obstetrical and gynecological diseases: toxemia of pregnancy, dysfunctional uterine bleeding, chronic pelvic infection, vaginal prolapse.

Qigong is contraindicated in acute infectious diseases, psychiatric diseases and in dyspneic conditions due to otolaryngeal diseases.

The Mechanism of *Qigong*

How *qigong* works remains uncertain. It has been postulated that *qigong* is a form of biofeedback. The signal from the patient itself is sent back to the patient to achieve self-regulation. In modern biofeedback therapy, both physiological and psychic, the signals of one's heart rate, blood pressure, electroencephalography and body temperature are picked up by electronic monitors, displayed and fed back to the patient for self-regulation. *Qigong* is similar to biofeedback treatment. A feeling of relaxation, calmness, warmth and heaviness may be experienced in either practice. The indications of *qigong* overlap those of biofeedback. Both treatments are effective in treating functional diseases. However, *qigong* does not require any equipment for the feedback of biological signals. The training of *qigong* allows an internal feedback mechanism to work. In other words, the biological signals or feelings are sensed by the body itself and are conveyed back to the body directly for self-regulation. On the contrary, modern biofeedback uses an external feedback mechanism. Signals need to be sensed by machines and then displayed to the patient for self-regulation purposes. The latter has the advantage of being easier to master. The drawback is that the biofeedback treatment is too expensive to make it popular. Aside from this difference, both forms of treatment are essentially the same.

Qigong is the training of the *qi*. Through voluntary, rhythmic, deep and lengthy breathing, one's oxygen consumption, blood pressure, heart rate, respiratory rate and serum lactate levels are reduced. It is not surprising then, that *qigong* is beneficial to autonomic system-related disorders.

The feeling of internal movement during *qigong* practice is called the movement of *internal qi*. Coinciding with the *qi* are infrared emission changes that one can see coming from the body. Research in China has shown that among patients with hypertension, those who practised *qigong* showed an increase in their infrared emissions compared with the control group. This is one piece of evidence suggesting that *qigong* may have a material basis.

Qigong masters who have studied the skill for many years not only can mobilize *qi* in the body, but may also emit it through the hands. Without touching the patient's body, *qi* may be emitted to the acupoints of a patient to induce a feeling of *arrival of the qi*. The patient may experience sensations such as numbness, heaviness, heat and distension. This *external qi*, which is believed to be a form of infrared ray, is detectable by special machines. How this form of *external qi* or *qigong* works and achieves therapeutic effect is still under investigation in China.